LAUGHING AT
POLITICAL CORRECTNESS

*How many light bulbs does it take
to change a liberal?*

D1715629

LAUGHING AT
POLITICAL CORRECTNESS

*How many light bulbs does it take
to change a liberal?*

by

DAVID COOK

LAUGHING AT
POLITICAL CORRECTNESS

World Ahead Press is a division of WND Books. The views and opinions expressed in this book are those of the author and do not necessarily reflect the official policy or position or WND Books.

Hardcover ISBN: 978-1-946918-12-3
eBook ISBN: 978-1-946918-13-0

Printed in the United States of America
16 17 18 19 20 21 LSI 9 8 7 6 5 4 3 2 1

DEDICATION

This book is dedicated to that half of America that recognizes the growing tyranny of political correctness— and the half that doesn't. But first, two caveats:

(1) If you found this book misfiled under "nonfiction," don't blame the author. "Nonfiction" is a section name in a bookstore, not a claim for truth. Even the election predictions of the *New York Times* qualify as "nonfiction."

(2) These chapters do not reflect the opinions of the author. Should anything prove politically incorrect, boycott someone else.

CONTENTS

4. Hansel and Gretel's Favorite Witch Recipes   58
   (PC is Hitler's legacy. Nothing justifies stifling opponents'
   free speech quite like mentioning Hitler's name, even as PC
   itself incites violence in America.)

5. Sacred Politics:
   The New Moral Majority   65
   (The old seven deadly sins slammed passions; the new seven
   deadlies, conservatives. The New Moral Majority looks for
   salvation in parades rather than the cross.)

6. Sleeping with Bill Cosby—The Routine That
   Ended Political Correctness   74
   (To hate Bill Cosby is to be a racist; to love him, to be a
   sexist. Guilty or not, Cosby, in his last comedy routine,
   ended his career and mercifully killed all dreams of universal
   PC.)

7. Crying "Fire!"   82
   (What are the limits of free speech? What are the limits of
   freedom of silence? Can a baker remain mute rather than
   discuss a wedding cake for a man and his pet sheep?)

8. Tolerance—Making the Sale, Not Buying
   the Belief   106
   Tolerating a shark attack demands no conversion to
   Zen Buddhism to "contemplate the sound of one hand
   clapping.")

9. The Equality Delusion   113
   (The delusion of equality is the opiate of PC. Laws can
   treat us equally, not make us equal. Only death brings true
   equality—and even then the air-conditioning may vary.)

8

EPIGRAPH

Almighty God hath created the mind free; that all attempts to influence it by . . . civil incapacitations tend only to beget habits of hypocrisy and meanness. . . . Truth is great, and will prevail if left to herself . . . she is the proper and sufficient antagonist to error, and has nothing to fear from the conflict, unless by human interposition disarmed of her natural weapons free argument and debate, errors ceasing to be dangerous when it is permitted freely to contradict them. . . .

—*Thomas Jefferson, 1786, American president, author, racist*

PREFACE

I wrote this book to laugh at the inconsistencies and feeble underpinnings of politically correct vocabulary. But is political correctness (PC) a laughing matter? On September 14, 2017, the two Houses of Congress passed Public Law 115-58, a joint resolution urging the President and his administration to—

    i) speak out against hate groups that espouse racism, extremism, xenophobia, anti-Semitism, *and* white supremacy [emphasis added].

    ii) use all resources available to the President and the President's Cabinet to address the growing prevalence of those hate groups in the United States . . .

I was relieved. The *and* in the resolution means that only groups that espouse *all* the no-no's qualify for hate. PC hardly allows defaming hate groups composed of African Americans, Jews, strangers, or extremists—especially if an "extremist" is defined as "one who is extremely against the wrong free speech." Still, one wonders: do the President's "resources" include nuclear weapons? Just in case, I suggest keeping your distance from white, conservative Christians and, to play it really safe, converting to Judaism and marrying a black Muslim.

I was saddened to learn, however, that the resolution urged the President to speak out against my own favorite hate group. Talk about sexists, racists, extremists, and white supremacists—this group is best known for fomenting and facilitating violence. Got to love 'em—even though were they alive today, Congress would reject them for "hateful expressions of intolerance that are contradictory to the values that define the people of the United States."[1] I am describing, of course, our Founding Fathers, who valued property, not PC, and thought nothing of their words giving offense. King George III did not call the traitors "offensive"; he called them "repugnant." Such is the response to those who treasure liberty.

Once the Bill of Rights forbad Congress to make laws abridging freedom of speech. Public Law 115-58 is apparently exempt from the rule—in spirit if not in word. The joint resolution doesn't actually ask the President to lock up people for overdoing freedom of speech. Instead the law pleads that the FBI investigate and collect data, just as they once collected data on Martin Luther King, Jr.—just in case.

Whatever the FBI's exact role, a group of concerned citizens protested Public Law 115-58, noting the law was passed *"without any public debate"* and was a bit shy on concrete definitions:

> These open-ended mandates to use the government to suppress groups associated with undefined sentiments like "hate group," "extremism," and "xenophobia" invite abuses of power by the state. They also legitimate and enable the aspiration of self-appointed arbiters of "hate," . . . to enlist Federal, state and local agencies in

stifling their political opponents' otherwise-protected free speech.²

The letter's concerns pretty much sum up this book. *Racism, sexism, nativism, homophobia, xenophobia, intolerance, conservative hate speech*—the words are nearly meaningless. As we will see, the borders distinguished by the words are too blurry to divide nature into true categories the way the term *cat* assures us the creature will not breed with dogs or platypuses. Nor do real categories change with perspective. Storks, frogs, spiders, coyotes—all are immune to the charms of the cat. In the vocabulary of PC, however, a white criticizing blacks is a "racist"; a black criticizing whites, a "victim." The terms created by PC revolve around groupthink, not logic, capturing human intercourse no better than a toddler's crayon captures the splendor of rainbows and butterflies.

The chapters that follow will explore, deconstruct, and expose the vocabulary of PC. We will argue, for instance, that the term *hate speech*—like Public Law 115-58—is nothing but politics masquerading as morality, nothing but an escalating tyranny demanding silence, abridging free speech, and stifling liberty.

INTRODUCTION

*Considering the chill of the author's prose, one could
hope he is now in a warmer place.*

—*Author's Epitaph*

B ehind every good man there is a good woman. Sometimes
more. Why are the good men always in front? Because
no woman with good sense would trust even the best of
men behind her. Mistakes occur. Accidents happen. Passions
intervene. Before we descend into political correctness (PC),
allow me to introduce the good women who have most helped
me to become what I am today—deplorable and proud.

MY THREE WIVES

My first wife was Jewish. She nurtured my love of Rosh
Hashanah, the Jewish New Year. I fondly recall it as the
religious holiday with the best food for the least praying. As
for those Passover Seders with her family, it would have been
enough to enjoy the four glasses of wine, but we nevertheless
enjoyed God's grace—there were no Baptists or Mormons
present, so we didn't have to drink grape juice.

I take full responsibility for the failure of that marriage. My
wife was perfect in every way but one: she had terrible taste in
husbands. Bless her heart! My wife, like Jesus, celebrated the

memory of the Exodus. The only sacred story that opens my heart is Jesus's own story. It shows what happens when you put even God in the hands of public opinion.

My current, third, and last—God and passion willing—wife is a Buddhist. Buddhists believe that we all suffer. Christians believe that we all sin. Since it is obviously more fun to sin than to suffer, Buddhism is likely to remain the minority religion.

I met my third wife when I traveled to Vietnam to celebrate the engagement party held in honor of our arranged marriage. Back then, we had a perfect relationship. Now she speaks English.

As I wrote in my novel *The Anatomy of Blindness*, "Half of all marriages don't work, and the other half are all work." But luckily, as my third marriage has proven, there are exceptions. Eight years into culinary bliss, I eat with chopsticks almost every night, and at times the curry chicken that manages to find my mouth rather than my tie puts even the Rosh Hashanah fare to shame.

Each night I pray to one day celebrate our golden wedding anniversary. That would get me to age 107. I'm afraid to ask for more. God might remember my first marriage.

As for my second wife, she was blond.

But enough about my wives. Enough about mutually cherished, uncoerced relationships, however fleeting. Enough about heartfelt confessions of appetites gone awry and then rehabilitated by chopsticks. Forget sincerity. Forget honesty. Forget about calling me a racist—unless you share the majority of your meals with someone of another race.

Let's get down to PC.

GETTING POLITICS—CORRECTLY

For most of my life I have been largely apolitical, voting in few elections, hazarding few political opinions, viewing politics as a noncontact sport—one having little if any contact with reality and certainly none with sincerity. Politics, I imagined, was like a soccer game in which lies are substituted for the ball. We cheer whenever our team gets another half-truth past the opposing team's goalie. We are as outraged by the other team's fallacies as we are irate when the blind referee tosses the penalty flag at our own.

So why consider politics now? There are two reasons for my sudden interest: one spawned by gratitude; the other, by righteous indignation.

First, the gratitude. In my book *Biomythology: The Skeptic's Guide to Charles Darwin and the Science of Persuasion*, I provided a training manual for recognizing how "science" is borrowed to sell values and politics. I described how scientific truth is the faith that future discoveries won't turn today's facts into tomorrow's fairytales such as "Once upon a time there were nine planets; then Pluto lost the vote." The only intelligent designs I mentioned were the rhetorical devices used by Darwin's disciples to sell his theory as the creation story of secular religion.

As it turned out, conservative radio stations across the nation interviewed me. The interviewers were great people, the kind I'd enjoy sharing dinner with: skeptics of groupthink. The liberals, however, apparently wanted no part in any blasphemy about science or cautions about confusing a possible road to truth with truth itself. I saw on which side my writer's bread was buttered and made the decision to support the group that supports me.

Period.

Now for the righteous indignation—the real reason for the book. In the past election, I grew weary of the press editing footage to position Hillary's professionally coached cheerleader smile against Trump's naturally earnest crusader scowl. I decided instead to vote for a first lady. There was no contest in my mind even though the *New York Times* used the science of probability to assure us that Bill Clinton had an 85 percent probability of becoming first lady (about the same numbers given when using the probability of global warming to sell beachfront property in Siberia). When Donald Trump defied political correctness to turn the *Time's* latest truth into yet another lie, I was reminded of the wisdom of *Charlotte's Web* author E. B. White upon Truman's surprise victory in 1948: "The total collapse of the public opinion polls shows this country is in good health. A country that developed an airtight system of finding out in advance what was in people's minds would be uninhabitable."[1]

Enheartened, I anticipated seeing our new First Lady modeling her inaugural ball gown. Then I read the hellfire and brimstone "Farewell America" sermon fresh from the digital pulpit of Bill Moyers. This secular evangelical assured me that "America died on Nov. 8, 2016" and that "the people chose a man who has shredded our values, our morals, our compassion, our dull tolerance, our decency, our sense of common purpose, our very identity." Forgetting that the American Revolution was fought and the nation conceived to protect property, not feelings, Moyers reduced my vote for Melania to the "the anger, the racism, the misogyny, the xenophobia, the nativism, the white sense of grievance." The group he assigned me to was pretty much plucked from

Hillary Clinton's "basket of deplorables": the racist, sexist, homophobic, xenophobic . . ., etc., etc., etc.

In the minds of Moyers, Clinton, and their ilk, the seven deadly good times—pride, greed, lust, anger, gluttony, envy, and sloth—have outlived their appeal. We need a new crop of sins concocted largely of isms and phobes: racism, sexism, nativism, homophobia, xenophobia, intolerance, and conservative hate speech. We need a new morality enforced by the New Moral Majority (NMM).

My only question for Bill Moyers is did he want to behold the spectacle of Bill Clinton standing at the urinal, hiking up a Vera Wang gown? But then Moyers is a disciple of Darwin and could doubtlessly quote me chapter, line, and verse of evolutionary psychology to prove natural selection favors cross-dressing because it makes genes less selfish and tell me that I was being politically incorrect for doubting it.

In truth, I got tired rather quickly of being bashed as deplorable—although months of studying the abuse being sold has since taught me to embrace my deplorability, to take pride in it. It turns out that the new seven deadlies are really much ado about nothing, merely political bells and whistles. Does sexism really cloud as many minds and break as many hearts as lust? Do the new sins really trump the old ones, or are they merely this year's social agreements, each shuffle of the deck of history qualifying as more enlightened than the previous cut of the cards? We are told that Scripture got morality all wrong for thousands of years. What lack of imagination makes us so sure that PC, with little track record at all, has it right this time? Have we replaced the sin of pride with the foolishness of out-and-out arrogance?

And what exactly is PC? Equality, racism, xenophobia, toleration, sexism—what do they really mean? The more I examine the vocabulary, the more I imagine that the terms have descended into unthinking groupthink of the NMM, a new Puritanism if you will, painfully more sanctimonious than the last.

So, gentle readers, stop listening. Think! The opiate of PC has become the delusion of equality. PC denies our spirituality, free will, and freedom of speech—all under the excuse of the same equality once peddled by the always-more-equal likes of Marx, Stalin, and Mao. Think! We should be treated equally under the law, but no law can make us equal. Think! If we were truly, truly equal, then there would be no need for bra sizes!

In the pages that follow, we will laugh as we deconstruct the joke of PC to reveal the illogic of its punch lines. May these chapters, like crocodile kisses, nibble away at an old ideology masquerading as a new grammar. The chains of PC attempt to bind not only our words but our souls. It is my sincerest wish that this polemic will release us from our bondage to politics masquerading as morality, that we may once more describe, without fear of character assassination or terror of loss of livelihood, what half of America is feeling in their hearts.

How many light bulbs does it take to change a liberal? We'll get there. Keep turning the pages until we meet in the basket to laugh at the deplorable truth.

CHAPTER 1

DEPLORABLE AND PROUD

Pride *goeth* . . . before a fall—but more frequently each
morning after arising.

—*Proverbs, et al.*

Deplorable and Proud—what kind of chapter title is that?
"Deplorable" sounds . . . well, deplorable! "Deplorable
and proud" sounds absolutely despicable! Well, sounds
can deceive. Forty years of work in exploring and expanding
the vision perception of patients has thoroughly convinced
me of the superiority of vision over other senses. Think
about it. If Mother Nature were to rebuild us from scratch,
forgetting a sense or two, would you prefer she gave you the
eye or the finger? When it comes to perception, equality is
strictly shunned. Vision rules the perceptual roost.

Historians agree. The father of Greek history, Herodotus,
wisely wrote, "Men trust their ears less than their eyes." And
well they should. In the words of Italian Renaissance historian
and political philosopher Niccolò Machiavelli, "Men judge
generally more by the eye than by the hand, because it belongs
to everybody to see you, to few to come in touch with you."
Still, Machiavelli recognized the potential aberrations of

optics: "Every one sees what you appear to be, few really know what you are."[1] Political correctness (PC) does what it can to reinforce this optical aberration of appearances over thought, hoping that appearances can overwhelm thought. Machiavelli might as well have called his little book *PC for Princes*.

Some have even suggested that Machiavelli himself was deplorable and proud, performing open-heart surgery on politics to reveal the famous malignancy, "the ends justify the means." He never said that of course. What he wrote was "in the actions of all men . . . one judges by the result." This advice provides the foundation for PC. If instead of championing equal protection under (and from) the law, we believe that segregation is inherently bad and that integration is inherently good, then the result of increasing the numbers of the integrated allows a favorable judgment on affirmative action and reverse discrimination even if they conflict with the concept of the same rule of law for all.

Under the rule of law, you see, we are all equal; that is, the identical law applies to one and all; we all get the same fine for the same speeding ticket. Under the rule of PC, laws treat some more equally than others. Because some minute percentage of Americans stem from forgotten ancestors who, by today's standards, misbehaved,[2] the school attended or job held may not necessarily match the SAT score or performance during the job interview. PC similarly counts some prejudices more equal than others, prejudice against black females being bad, prejudice against white males being good, prejudice against white straight Christian conservative males being the best! In other words, quotas judge prejudice according to the color of its skin. In this way, PC—judging actions by their results in creating equality even where none in reality exists—exemplifies the political philosophy of Niccolò Machiavelli.

If you believe that the logic of PC is not sound, but noise, join me. Instead of listening to the creed of the New Moral Majority (NMM), use your eyes. Machiavelli would agree; a picture is worth a thousand lies. Visualize, juggle the images in your mind, as we paint the deplorable picture of what PC forbids us to hear and how it legislates for us whom we must "come in touch with."

HUMAN PREJUDICE AND RIGHTS

Existing outside of time, God prefers truth to probability. Blind to transcendence, science prefers probability to God. Only the scientific-minded lived with an 85 percent chance of sunshine, clouds, or Hillary on election day. Then November 8, 2016, arrived to shake history free from the illusion of probability. The probability of Hillary's success plummeted into truth—zero.

As we look back, is it logical that Trump really had a 15 percent chance of victory one day and a 100 percent chance of victory the next? Did the truth change on election day, or is the distance between yesterday's probability and today's truth but a measure of human fallibility and prejudice?

Science assures us that the bullet, aimed according to the laws of physics, will hit the bull's-eye. Period. When blundering into human consciousness, however, the aim of science falters. Instead of a bull's-eye, science settles for a bell curve. Soon, prejudice becomes the bell curve blinding us to the curves of the belle. Thus, the probabilities of the *New York Times* blinded many to Hillary's bottle blondness. Such is the penalty for placing prejudice before perception.

Although scientists use probability to turn prejudice into a science if not an art form, we are all prejudiced. It's how we see. Having taught thousands of souls to use their eyes for school and sports, let me assure you: seeing is something we do, not something that happens to us. Despite the gospel of the same basic science class that taught us that there were nine planets, we are not slaves of the light rebounding from the neural trapeze nets at the backs of our eyes. Rather we see according to the prejudices learned during the dance of our eyes with former exploration and action. Such prejudice washes the windows to the soul. We see what habit has taught us to expect, what life has taught us to value.[3]

Without such prejudice, we are blind. The vision of infants, for instance, is free from this prejudice, but then infants can't see poop—especially during that period when their parents find themselves seeing little else. Prejudice, however, has its liabilities. We create illusions when we export to new surroundings vision learned by actions in former surroundings: the straight sticks we held on dry land magically bend as they pierce water; the proximity of rainbows defies confirmation from the swiftest chase.

Is the glass half empty or half full? The prejudice of our perceptions reflects our souls as truly as a mirror. Those with full hearts see the glass as half full; those with empty heads see the glass as half empty. In a world in which deplorability and PC are but two ends of the same spectrum, we are deemed *deplorable* if our full hearts applaud the full half of the glass. Nature, proclaiming her "natural rights," however, always stacks the empty half of the glass on top. Mimicking nature, PC edits language to allow only the emptiest words to the top of the debate.

Yes, PC is big on natural rights. According to the *Declaration of Independence*, "Nature's God," the "Creator" provided the "Laws of Nature," not to mention "self-evident" and "inalienable rights." Amusingly, those who continue to dream up the greatest number of natural, inalienable rights—the inalienable right to eat without a need to work, the natural right to victimize others to pay for the health and child care consequences of our "victimless" crimes—can't wait to get God expelled from the courthouse and public park. When it comes to rights, ignoring God is dicey. Unless we are mixing metaphors, the rights of spiritual beings are created by their Creator, not Nature. Mother Nature selects, she does not create. If we can reduce divine law to the laws of physics, what's to prevent us from reducing human rights to the rights of molecules?

Toss out faith in God and what's left? Choose your faith. Faith in probability? Faith in passion? Faith in rhetorical reason? Faith in groupthink? Faith in Machiavellian pragmatism? Faith in politics? And so, we hear the chorus, "It is most probable that . . ." "It just feels right." "The reason is sound." "Everybody thinks so." "It worked . . . at least for now (at least for me)." And, "Our political action committee won!" Such are the less-than-certain justifications providing the foundation of our rights in a secular society. Like a house built on sand, our imagined natural rights wait to be washed away with each discovery or whim changing the fashions of science or philosophy. To experience "natural" rights, try swimming in a tsunami.

These metaphors of natural human rights may be sophisticated if not downright deplorable. No matter. In a world of relative morality, deplorability is in the dictionary of the beholder. My health coach finds chocolate to be deplorable. As I finish my ice cream cone and lick the last of the chocolate from my fingers, I find deplorable is beautiful.

Language evolves. Once science borrowed *atoms* from the Greeks as "uncuttable"! Today, science gaily cuts the exact same uncuttable *atoms* into a zoo of particles. Truth is unchangeable. The stories told by science and philosophy are not. We can kill a thousand secular stories with a single discovery—or a string of political victories. Take the word *gay.* Once it denoted "joy and mirth." Today, thanks to grassroots politics fertilized by overflow from the wrong creek, *gay* now modifies "rights." Before we finish this book, I hope we have enough votes to elect *deplorable* to fill the vacuum in laughter created by replacing joy and mirth with the fleeting success of the politics of perversion.[4]

Consider yet a different metaphor. Freedom is a coin. Toss it and you'll find freedom *to* on one side, freedom *from* on the other. The deplorable prefer freedom *to*—freedom *to* toil, *to* produce, *to* pray, *to* speak our minds, *to* dream, freedom *to* pursue property. PC more often champions freedom *from*—freedom *from* want, *from* speech, *from* prayer, *from* discrimination, freedom *from* truth—and most importantly, freedom *from* conservatives.

If this strikes you as a one-sided argument about a two-sided coin, I won't disagree. Still, having defined "deplorable" well enough for our purposes, we need only defend *pride* to justify the *Deplorable and Proud* of this chapter's title.

PRIDE

Although my sins are hardly more original than the next guy's, I formerly tried to steer clear of pride—one of the seven deadly sins, you know—at least until the NMM revised the list to delete pride. If the new parades are any indication, our lusts and fetishes are now something to take pride in rather than to bury beneath "free excuse": it was a mistake; it was dark; I was drunk; the devil in my genes made me do it!

If Jane Austin were to write *Pride and Prejudice* today, any New York editor worth her dedication to free speech would blue-pencil *Prejudice* to protect the sense and sensibilities of an impressionable reading public arrogantly deemed by the publishing industry to be too stupid to discriminate for themselves. Even though we would be blind as infants without it, prejudice—another "freedom to"—is deplorable. It's out. Pride is in. So, join me in being deplorable and proud.

CARVING GROUPTHINK AT THE SYNAPSES

Happily, the new seven deadly sins, racism, sexism, nativism, homophobia, xenophobia, intolerance, and conservative hate speech, continue to share space with "deplorable" in the dictionary of the beholder. Amusingly, we will find that the definitions of the new deadlies—fabricated to terrorize into silence the politically incorrect—do not carve nature at the joints;[5] they carve groupthink at the synapses. In this polemic, we will deconstruct the lexicon of PC in order to declare our deplorable freedom of speech and share our deplorable minds while they are still our own rather than dictated by factions seeking to control communication in order to control minds. Before we proceed, however, allow me to sketch out a few warnings lest those milking tears from offense show up crying on my digital doorstep to short out, virtually speaking, my deplorable heart.

A CAVEAT ON STRAW-MAN RACISM

The last time you called your health insurance company, before you spoke to a living person, remember that prerecorded voice warning you that anything the representative said could be a lie, and that if the elective surgery didn't kill you, the bill might? We call such a warning a caveat. We'll end this chapter with a few caveats of our own.

First, don't blame me if some idiot borrows my arguments to justify committing atrocities or shouting obscenities at those without the faculties to ignore them or realize the obscenities define the shouters, not the hearers.[6] That would be as dumb as blaming Jesus for waterboarding and Columbine because the Golden Rule gives every pain-seeker with a death wish a license for torture and mass murder. As George Bernard Shaw wrote, "Do not do unto others as you would that they do unto you. Their tastes may not be the same."[7]

To say that "the race is not to the swift" is religion. To say the race "is not too swift" is racism—especially if you are an Asian American laughing at the standardized test-taking abilities of half-witted European Americans such as me. Once racists were made of flesh and blood and sporting whips, hounds, nooses, torches, and bricks. Today's racists are more often made of straw. The straw-man term fallaciously appeals to emotion by conjuring images of flaming crosses whenever someone chooses inconvenient words, beliefs, or politics deemed unfit by PC. I don't know about you, but I never carry a cigarette lighter, much less a flaming cross. Confusing violence, the direct threat of violence, or the direct intent to incite violence with straw-man racism is nothing but equivocation—linguistic bait and switch, if you will—confusing the definitions of words for the purpose of deceit.

We will deal with "race" and "racism" in detail in chapter 12 as, one by one, we deconstruct the NMM's seven deadly sins. For now, just think of "racist" as the r-word replacing the n-word. The r and n words both are used to promote the superiority of the speaker. Both are calculated to dehumanize people while spurring political agendas. Both intimate the terror of damaged property or livelihood as the penalty for failing to remain silent or vanish. Both spread the contagion of hate needed to assault liberal protestors or conservative politicians. Both tell us more about the insecurities of the speaker than the inferiorities of the target. While the n-word extends the injustice of the past into the present, the r-word rests on balancing the scales of justice between historical time zones, on punishing those who were children or yet unborn when the drama of little people using big government to preserve the economic, political, and social status quo was performed.

My suggestion? When history is cited, look for an argument concocted to justify passion. Reduced to a rhetorical device, history plays the role of a "jealous God, visiting the iniquity of the fathers upon the children unto the third and fourth generation." See the rhetoric for what it is: a sales pitch.

If those who hope to exclude your voice from the political debates and empower a new elite have twisted your words and heart to declare you a racist, it's time to became deplorable and proud. There is no justification for denying your humanity just because you love bigots such as George Washington, Thomas Jefferson, or Abraham Lincoln.[8] These founders and preservers of our nation provide dead proof that being a racist need not outweigh your contributions to humanity—at least until the deniers of politically incorrect history get the faces of Washington and Lincoln scissored from our banknotes and the Jefferson Memorial demolished or, possibly, rededicated as a temple to diversity.

If your racism is made of straw, I hope you find the founding-fathers metaphor useful for breaking down the thoughtless stereotypes that thoughtless people thoughtlessly apply to dishonor you. Violence, terror, cruelty, or unequal protection under the law—these are the real problems, not racial preference. To treat others as we want to be treated is enough. We need not exchange our children for those of a different race. I prefer my Asian wife, and nothing short of polygamy could turn me into an equal opportunity husband.

No matter what PC argues, trees are responsible for more lynchings than are off-colored jokes. If PC can nevertheless march to save the trees, the words of this polemic can march to save our reputations and livelihoods from fantasized isms and phobias.

CHAPTER 2

HOW MANY LIGHT BULBS DOES IT TAKE
TO CHANGE A LIBERAL?

The difference between the almost right word and the
right word is really a large matter—it's the difference
between the lightning bug and the lightning.

—*Mark Twain*

One of the most basic characteristics of conscious and
unconscious life is *discrimination*, "the perception of
a difference between two stimuli, esp. as evidenced by
a different reaction to each." Plants discriminate between
light and darkness, growing toward the sun, not the shade.
Amoebae behave differently in the presence of toxins than
sugar. Those with intelligence greater than a plant or an
amoeba similarly find themselves capable of discrimination,
of seeing differences and adjusting behavior accordingly.

In the world of political correctness (PC), however,
discrimination is an evil, an unnatural act. Substituting
ideology for observation, PC demands uniform behavior
toward all. Like a two-year-old unaware of doll color, like
a four-year-old largely unable to recognize the difference

between the letters *b* and *d*, PC confuses diversity with equality, right with left, discrimination with prejudice.

Not all discriminations are equal, as we will examine when, below, we learn how many light bulbs it takes to change a liberal. In the meantime, let's take a look at the intricacies and sensitivities of that new grammar of PC with its insistence on twisting and weaving exotic words—homophobia, xenophobia—out of the straw of Greek in much the same manner as clinical groupthink derived the umbrella term *dyslexia* to turn a lack of reading talent into reimbursable diagnosis code and a handicap in the academic horserace. Still, never underestimate the power of Greek. The *isms* or *phobias* of the new grammar can get your reputation electrocuted quicker than your confusing a lightning *bolt* for a lightning *bug*.

WHAT DO YOU CALL SOMEONE WHO . . .

We will warm up by practicing our PC. What do we call someone who gets our seatback in the upright position on a jet flight: a stewardess, a flight attendant, or a mile-high-club fantasy come true? What do we call the guy who collects the garbage: a garbage person, a sanitary engineer, or a husband? What do we call a former American slave: a Negro, a Black, or an African American?

And more difficult still, what do we call an African American who emigrates from America to England: an African American Englishman, a British African American, or an American British African? Does nativism make any difference? Does citizenship matter? Should we call him a human being, or would that, in Mark Twain's eyes, qualify us as racists for demeaning the emigrant as a member of the human race? Should we instead call him an animal to proclaim his equality with all species of the animal kingdom? Or should we call him a vegetable to put the animal-kingdomists in their place and remind us that all life forms are equal?

The politically correct answer is simple. Unless we want to end up in big trouble, we should call him whatever he wants to be called. If our half-black-half-white past president calls himself African American, we should call him that too.

For instance, I'm an optometrist,[1] a minority member of a healthcare community dominated by medical supremacists.[2] When I entered the profession four decades ago, optometrists were forbidden to lease space in medical buildings or publish in medical journals. The medical supremacists used to distribute a pamphlet, *The Pen*, to members of Congress, educating them on the inferiority of the optometric subspecies. The supremacists also wrote "scientific" position statements denying the major contributions of our profession in increasing human perceptual ability. A few years back, we were even discussed in one of their "scientific" journals. The cover was filled with the image of a duck.

Things are changing, but prejudices die hard. Optometrists are still forbidden to attend educational programs at medical supremacist academy meetings. Indeed, a few months ago, a local supremacist summed it up when he informed one of my patients, "I am a doctor. He is a quack!"

Oh! The q-word. Be still my outraged heart! As if I were hypnotized, the beat of the q-word against my eardrums triggers my irrational behavior, transforming me into a quivering mass of perplexed protoplasm unable to breathe, much less maintain detached reasoning skills or logical argumentation. I am a hopeless victim of sound waves—or maybe a victim of those who promote my victimization by sound waves, those who daily revile the q-word to magnify its force beyond the trembling of air in the hopes of keeping me emotionally immobilized.

Or not.

From forty years of experience watching my profession evolve under the pressure of misinformation and bigotry, I can tell you that—without binding the human tongue to edit freedom of speech, without borrowing PC to banish the q-word, and without a fiat of law demanding equality—there are different ways to deal with prejudice, and these I will cover in my next-to-last chapter.

For now, suffice it to say that despite the supremacists' dream to eliminate us from the kingdom of healthcare, if not the face of the earth, I continue to flourish and prosper. My professional papers appear in peer-reviewed journals and in 1998, 2004, and 2016 won journal awards for best articles of the year. I am invited to speak across the nation and world. I have served on a national optometric political board and on both national and international examination boards of my profession. Patients have come to me from throughout the nation, not to mention England and Germany—fortunately not at the same time. Optometrists across the nation have distributed close to forty thousand copies of my first book, *When Your Child Struggles*.[3]

To fixate someone's attention on their victimization is the cruelest and most insidious form of victimization. It's as cruel as giving patients diagnoses to live up to. They become their "attention deficit disorders." If the diagnosis inspires the patient to work harder, fine. But if, instead, patients live out their diagnoses, then we are talking about not diagnoses but excuses to fail.

To paraphrase the poet, we can't stop the rain by complaining.[4] I am, therefore, too busy to remove myself from the game while I waste time buying into my victimization by medical supremacists. I wouldn't consider reducing my services to their level so I can be "equal." I specialize in treating children and adults with reading problems or difficulty with two-eye depth perception. For these patients, I am not as good as a supremacist. In my mind at least, I am better. Sure, supremacists have not only their weaknesses, but their strengths. They provide superior service in many areas of eye care, and I refer patients to them, but the only relationship that matters is not with the supremacists but with my patients.

While the supremacists, when not using the q-word, call me "Mister," my patients generally call me "Doctor." Indeed, when a child calls me "Mr. Cook," the parent corrects the child to say, "Dr. Cook." My response: "That's okay. You don't have to call me Dr. Cook. You may call me, 'Your Highness.'"

For the purposes of this polemic, you may also call me "Your Highness." If you want to be politically correct, that is. My preference is your command. Otherwise don't get your underwear in a wad if I substitute the word *mankind* for *humankind* or call God "He" instead of "He-She-It." Who cares if a few Oxy Morons[5] want to change the pronouns of the English language to keep the outliers from falling off the end of the sexual bell curve? If you won't call me "Your Highness," then forget about the enlightenment of pronouns. *He* and *his* will have to suffice. I will continue with an earlier tradition, a tradition that preferred good grammar to what now counts as good taste—the ghost of a slogan that returns me to my past.

When I was a child watching a small black-and-white TV screen in an enormous blond veneer cabinet, the most famous advertising jingle was, "Winston tastes good like a cigarette should." In time, the grammatical purists complained that the slogan should be edited to "Winston tastes good *as* a cigarette should." In response, Winston retorted with a new jingle, "What do you want? Good grammar or good taste?" In this book, I promise neither. We are going to question the agreements of today's grammar of political correctness, and I will try to be as tasteless as I can without being pilloried by the new grammarians.

Humor is the collision between a better place and this one. In that better place, the real is indistinguishable from the ideal; words say what they mean and mean what they say. In this world, we are forbidden to say what we mean or mean what we say. We call this disconnect between word and meaning PC.

DISCRIMINATION FOR ALL

Take the term *discriminate*, which came into use in the 1620s, and its earliest definition (def. 1) was "to perceive the difference in or between." For instance, those who can *discriminate* between the tiniest differences are said to be the most discriminating. Or, if we are unable to *discriminate* between the presence and absence of light we are stone-cold blind; we lack "light perception."

Discrimination (def. 1) has lost favor. Many people will misunderstand the statement, "Only a fool is incapable of discrimination." Why? Beginning in 1866, possibly to help commemorate or justify the greatest slaughter of American life in history, definition two (def. 2) began to win over the popular vote. *Discrimination* now became a political rather than a perceptual term meaning "prejudice or injustice against people based on grounds of race or color." Gradually, the list of banned prejudices has been extended to include social status, religion, gender, sex, age, fashion sense, political party, ability, and ideology. For instance, "It is politically incorrect to *discriminate* against the depth of handicaps or the height of trousers." "It is politically correct to *discriminate* against those in 'the basket of deplorables.'"

As any homeschool parent knows, teaching children can be a challenge. When adjusting the lesson plan to the child, it is sometimes difficult to know if the child *won't* learn the lesson or *can't*. Discriminating between "won't" and "can't" is part of what makes a teacher a teacher. The same holds true for working with the politically correct. Sometimes it is next to impossible to tell those who won't discriminate (def. 2) from those who can't discriminate (def. 1), which brings us to our light-bulb joke.

Question: How many light bulbs does it take to change a liberal?

Answer: Don't waste the electricity. The politically correct neither may, nor can, discriminate whether the light is on or off. Try electroconvulsive therapy.

As PC knows, the only way to end discrimination is to forbid perception—or to forbid spoken images of perception, a sort of verbal iconoclasm. The road to equality for red and green marbles is paved with neither educational opportunity nor integration, but camouflage or color blindness.

DEPLORABLE ARGUMENTS

That said, our polemic will argue a number of other points, all of which possess their own ambiguities, their own paradoxes, their own calls for opposing viewpoints.[6] We will argue, for instance, that marching for African American rights, women's rights, or gay rights are but bids for the political power of groups whose members secretly believe themselves to be somehow inferior to, superior to, or exempt from the human race. Otherwise, the marches would champion merely *human* rights.

We will argue that all are equal in the eyes of God and should be in the eyes of the law, but if we were equal in the eyes of men, the scales of justice would work and the scale in the bathroom would not have to.

We will argue that once we were proud to be Americans. Now special interests come first, then America. Asian Americans, African Americans, Hispanic Americans, LBGTQ Americans, and, like me, European Americans—the adjectives subtract from, not add to, being pure and unadulterated "Americans." Kind of like "Asian pregnant" or "African pregnant" or "a-little-bit pregnant"—the modifiers are superfluous, adding nothing of importance to the ultimate purpose and consequence of the condition.

We will deconstruct, or demolish if you will, the seven deadly sins of the NMM—racism, sexism, nativism, homophobia, xenophobia, intolerance, and conservative hate speech—arguing that the terms stand for beliefs, not sins, provide the infrastructure for a hate speech all their own, and prove about as logically coherent and safe as speeding down a one-way street whose direction of flow varies by sex or ethnicity. Not surprisingly, collisions are bound to occur.

We will argue that love is never a sin, although kissing may be. Loving our own children more than we love a president's children is not a sin. Love of race, gender, religion, or country is not a sin.

We will similarly argue that hatred of human beings is always a sin. Whether directed at African Americans, women, or the basket of deplorables—hatred is hatred. To hate a man's idea does not justify hating or generating hatred against the man—even if he is African American, Christian, or President Trump.

We will argue that hate speech is hate speech but that hate speech is the price we must pay for free speech. Madonna said, "Yes, I'm angry. Yes, I am outraged. Yes, I have thought an awful lot about blowing up the White House."[7] We are blessed to live in a country where even Madonna has free speech. Naked hatred, however, is hatred whether dressed up with the words of a liberal celebrity or dressed down as too conservative for the kingdom of PC.

We will argue that the labels of politically sanctioned groups (gay, Hispanic, European American, etc.) are too often used as curtains behind which to hide. As Mark Twain wrote, "Man is the only animal that blushes. Or needs to." The tragedy of racism is that it dehumanizes, opening the door to violence and abuse. But our faults are what make us truly human; robots never sweep the dust beneath the rug. What could dehumanize a race quicker than to claim its members have no need to blush? Such embellishments are racism pure and simple.

We will argue that God's greatest gift is relationship, and our most basic God-given right is to accept or reject a relationship—with Him, or anyone else. If you don't have to kiss God, you certainly don't have to kiss the Frog Prince—even if that kiss could ultimately win you a kingdom. Avoiding the kiss may be the biggest mistake of *your* life. Pining for *your* kiss may be the stupidest mistake of the *frog's* life. But forbidding you to duck as the frog's fly-gobbling tongue unfolds in your direction like a squeaking party favor is little different than legitimizing rape. "Just say no!" is no protection when you can't say, "No!"

Finally, we will argue that God created us with free will and provided us with a roadmap for choosing a path. PC tosses the roadmap, denies our free will, and instead dreams of making all the paths equal so our illusionary choices won't matter—especially since all secular paths converge to the same destination: a dead end.

Anyway, that's my story—well, my polemic. Every story has two sides, a polemic only one. As an author, it's not my job to buy these unbalanced arguments, only to sell them. If you want to develop better balance, throw away this book and buy a trampoline. If, however, you would rather avoid physical exercise, join me instead on the moral tightrope walk provided by the chapters that follow.

CHAPTER 3

LAUGHING AT
POLITICAL CORRECTNESS

If the man doesn't believe as we do, we say he is a
crank, and that settles it. I mean, it does nowadays,
because now we can't burn him.

—*Mark Twain*

Political correctness (PC) is hypocrisy. In America,
hypocrisy is nothing new. "In 1790, United States
government figures showed that annual per-capita
alcohol consumption for everybody over fifteen amounted
to thirty-four gallons of beer and cider, five gallons of
distilled spirits, and one gallon of wine."[1] Both religious
and secular colonial authorities condemned inebriation, the
Bible classifying drunkenness under "lust of the flesh," Ben
Franklin agreeing that "nothing is more like a fool than a
drunken man." As our nation was born, PC demanded we
learn to hold our liquor, feigning sobriety. Today PC demands
we hold our tongues, feigning support for the abridgement
of freedom of speech once promised by our Bill of
Rights.

The Bill of Rights protects our speech from oppression by the federal government; PC protects our speech from oppression by logic. Despite Twain's optimism, the "crank" now enjoys immunity from fire, but no protection from dehumanization, no relief from silencing, no respite from the boycott. As this and the chapters that follow will argue, the flames of PC rage as never before, consuming liberty, burning away a freedom that no delusion of equality can restore.

As explained in 1859 by philosopher John Stuart Mills:

> Men might as well be imprisoned as excluded from the means of earning their bread. Those whose bread is already secured, and who desire no favors from men in power, or from bodies of men, or from the public, have nothing to fear from the open avowal of opinions.[2]

Since Mill's day, public opinion remains as fickle as ever. We willingly trade freedom of speech for freedom of boycott. Celebrity chef Paula Dean, for instance, used the n-word; Wal-Mart, Target, and Kmart, to name a few, couldn't sever business relations with her quickly enough for comfort, demoting the vocabulary of her recipes to secondary importance. Sure, in America we can still speak our minds, but only if we don't mind a store.

ABHORRING VACUUMS

So why does nature abhor vacuums and political correctness (PC)? Both forbid sound to travel. PC has become the ingenious secular creed espoused by the New Moral Majority (NMM). How can religion be secular, you may ask? If PC can turn diversity into equality, then oxymoron is hardly limited to the Oxy Morons. Relative morality reduces to one absolute: conservatives are deplorable. A fresh skepticism is needed to face the intolerance of a NMM with its freshly created deadly sins strangely overlooked by most of mankind throughout most of history.

The last chapter's confusions of language are not the only source of humor. Humor also fills the gap between being human and being humane. Mark Twain built a career on observing the gap, writing, "Etiquette requires us to admire the human race."

PC, I fear, is the new etiquette commanding us to censor language in the hope we will come to admire those no less human, or more admirable, than ourselves. Can changing the language without changing the speakers of the language really change anything? Can calling an egg an *unhatched visitor* reduce the beatings or improve a tasteless dish without actually changing the recipe of the omelet? Can rewriting a language make all dogs equal, a canine species no longer including alphas, just betas, no more studs and bitches—just virginally conceived, playful puppies cramped into a utopian kennel? Instead of teething on kibble, can the pups survive on a diet of ideological dribble?

PC is rampant intolerance of intolerance: the politically correct's intolerance of the politically incorrect—those intolerant of the wrong *particular* groups and politics. In the same sense, this polemic thrives on intolerance of the politically correct, my words exemplifying intolerance of intolerance of intolerance, those intolerant of this book similarly proving intolerant of intolerance of intolerance of intolerance. PC, it turns out, is the intolerance voted most likely to succeed.

Confused? Don't worry. PC is confusing. It's like a jigsaw puzzle whose pieces mesh only when facedown, the puzzle's enchantment being lost to all but those who, like the tabletop, stand woodenly beneath its spell.

DANCING WITH POLITICAL CORRECTNESS

I am far from alone in my skepticism about PC. Hal Holbrook, who onstage often played the part of Mark Twain, confessed, "I got a feeling about political correctness. I hate it. It causes us to lie silently instead of saying what we think."

Having experienced the hypocrisy of PC, I agree. My dad was born in the South in 1899; his mother never forgot how the Yankees had "thrown their corn in the creek." My mother was born to two Swedish immigrants in the farmland outside of Chicago in 1912. Both my parents had eighth-grade educations. My mother was forced to drop out of school at age fourteen to work for a pittance as a servant for a wealthy family; my father wandered the hobo jungles before joining the Navy and learning to obey the signs posted in naval towns, "Sailors and Dogs Keep off the Grass." Both my parents were bigots after the fashion of their times, but my mother had a natural bent for PC. She studiously avoided the n-word and was careful—for my edification, I suppose—to correct my father when, in front of me, his PC faltered. It was not until I was a teenager, though, that I saw how things really stood.

One evening at a high-school party, I met Linda, a Seminole Indian. We slow danced. As passions stirred, we kissed. Sure, I had kissed my mother in the past, but as attested by my tonsils, Linda did not kiss like my mother. Satan, I imagine, had to get behind me, because Linda was pressed too tightly against my front for approach from that direction. The electricity generated by my heart, and sundry other organs, jolted my person from head to toe, shorting out the receptor cells in my eyes to leave me blind to color, decorum, and any faintest taint of decency. Before the dance was over, I asked Linda to the prom. She accepted, contingent on my ability to win the blessings of her parents.

Linda, it turned out, was adopted, her parents black,[3] their home small but tidy, a picture of Jesus supervising the frayed throw rugs on the living room's hardwood floor. For some reason, the parents immediately, and correctly, assumed I was after only one thing. As they interrogated me, I centered my responses on the topic of dancing, fiercely avoiding any mention of the fantasized future rituals scalding conscience and consciousness.

The couple prodded my intentions for some time, nailing down the exact schedule of prom night. When I got home to an apartment even tinier than Linda's home, I told my parents about the unwarranted (not!) interrogation. My mother looked no happier than Linda's parents, but rather than confess her obvious dissatisfaction with my choice of dance partner, turned her upset to the couple who had doubted the integrity of her son (who at that point had none). Mom's resentment, indignation, and, yes, hatred, seemed to fill the room, but nary a mention of race passed her politically correct lips. My politically incorrect father, on the other hand, only laughed and asked, "Did they offer you a piece of watermelon?"

By the superficial standards of today's PC, Dad, not Mom, would qualify as "the racist." Yet only Dad was aware of the wisdom of the black parents' skepticism, careful interrogation, and keen effort to remove any troublesome opportunities from the evening. Despite his political incorrectness, he saw those parents (and me) as all too human, and unlike my mother's politically correct heart, his was not filled with petty hatred.

The summer before my senior year of high school, Dad died of a stroke, the Lord, if PC has anything to say about Divine Justice, taking him for his political incorrectness. Despite his penchant for speaking his mind rather than worrying about PC, a hundred friends attended his funeral. When my politically correct mother died twenty years later, only my brother and I were there. I would be willing to bet that there was more affection in my father's off-color jokes than there is humor in the hearts of those with zero toleration for the n-word and not a care about dehumanizing their rivals with the r-word.[4] All hate speech is equal, but in the world of PC some hate speech is more equal than others. Seeing how my father actually treated those before him, I learned to believe that actions speak louder than words. Like Hal Holbrook, I hate political correctness, and so would anyone else who really cared to know what was on others' minds.

As this anecdote reveals, I am not responsible for my political incorrectness. My genome and upbringing, both inherited from my father, make me do it. It's my free excuse and I'm sticking with it.

To judge people by words rather than actions is, in my eyes, chancy. As in our opening chapter, we can readily see the debt that PC owes to the great Italian political philosopher Niccolò Machiavelli, who assured us "it is unnecessary for a prince to have all the good qualities . . . but it is very necessary to appear to have them." Such is the nature of PC: wholesale endorsement of Machiavellianism. Machiavelli, also anticipating PC, wrote that "a prince ought to take care that he never lets anything slip from his lips that . . . [would make him appear not to be] merciful, faithful, humane, upright, and religious. There is nothing more necessary to appear to have than this last quality."[5] The appearance of such religiosity applies tenfold when publicly adhering to the creed of the NMM.

Nobel Laureate Doris Lessing wrote, "Politcal correctness is the natural continuum from the party line. What we are seeing once again is a self-appointed group of vigilantes imposing their views on others. It is a heritage of communism, but they don't seem to see this."[6] Lessing is historically correct. Political correctness once emerged "in Communist terminology as a policy concept denoting the orthodox party line of Chinese Communism as enunciated by Mao Tse Tung in the 1930s."[7] It seems that the party line is winning under the name of PC even if it lost under the name of communism.[8] PC has reversed the flow of the McCarthy communist witch hunts of the 1950s. Indeed, if socialism is an economic system and communism a political system, then PC is the oppression of language lowering socialism into communism. Continuing the hyperbole, PC's suppression of free speech moves us ever closer to creating a turnkey operation for tyrants.

Elsewhere Lessing captured the insidiousness of PC more completely:

> The most powerful mental tyranny in what we call the free world is Political Correctness, which is both immediately evident, and to be seen everywhere, and as invisible as a kind of poison gas, for its influences are often far from the source, manifesting as a general intolerance.[9]

Continuing this theme of tyranny, Academy Award winner Charlton Heston provided the frank and true aphorism, "Political correctness is tyranny with manners." Indeed, in PC we find the slippery slope of progress headed toward the blind precipice of despotism.

But PC is apparently not for everyone. How come, you may ask, some groups can hide behind the mask of PC while others can't? Did not author George Orwell, in *Animal Farm*, capture the spirit of PC when he wrote of communism, "All animals are equal, but some animals are more equal than others." Are some groups similarly more "equal" than others? Does PC come with an agenda other than strict equality? For that matter, what exactly does PC have to do with "equality"? We will ponder such questions in later chapters.

In the meantime, although it is far from politically correct to say so, guns don't kill people, people kill people. Words don't lie. People lie. From this perspective, burying guns and words to eliminate violence and lies is vanity. First, we bury the guns, then the words. Then we discover that nothing less than burying the people can set things right.

PC is just the first step toward that graveyard known as Utopia. The goal of PC is equality, and as it has been and will be said many times (repeatedly in just these chapters, for instance), we are equal only in death. Utopia promises a true state of equality—humanity without the embarrassment of humans. Whenever a group's bid for power uses utopian dreams to curtail freedom of speech, it's time to wake up. It's time to become deplorable and proud before the nightmare really gets started.

DICTIONARY PC

As we shake the sleep from our eyes, let's explore a different set of viewpoints on PC, turning to the authors of dictionaries as they sample language, dipping their lexicographic ladles into the stream of groupthink.

The Living Dictionary of the Oxy Morons tells us that PC is "the avoidance of forms of expression or action that are perceived to exclude, marginalize, or insult groups of people who are socially disadvantaged or discriminated against." PC thus rests on perception, not facts. When discriminating between the virtues of individual group members, it is apparently safer to save our powers of discrimination for separating the wheat from the chaff within groups damned for their advantages—the "basket of deplorables" for instance (God love us!). As an authority well acquainted with how often visual perception lies, my professional opinion is that the definition holds water about as well as a drunk passed out in a gutter.

Merriam Webster Learner's Dictionary tells us that PC is "agreeing with the idea that people should be careful to not use language or behave in a way that could offend a *particular* group of people" (emphasis added). PC is once again an agreement, an idea, an ideology, not a fact. Since the definition was written for children or learners of a second language, it does not explain the particular meaning of *particular*, but evidently conservatives are not *particular* enough to qualify.

Merriam-Webster for grownups suggests that PC is all about "conforming to a belief that language and practices which could offend political sensibilities (as in matters of sex or race) should be eliminated." Here the definition has evolved from an idea to conformation to a belief. Again, no facts are mentioned. We remain in the realm of opinion—because logic could hardly explain why offending "political sensibilities" would not include promoting socialism to offend the sensibilities of libertarians.

At Cambridge, PC is "avoiding language or behavior that any *particular* group of people might feel is unkind or offensive" (emphasis added). Again, feelings not facts. In words attributed to Thomas Paine, "He who dares not offend cannot be honest." Similarly, Nigerian author Chimamanda Ngozi Adichie writes in her novel *Half of a Yellow Sun,* "The truth has become an insult." So, let's eliminate from political debate any truth or honesty allowing insult or offense. This will give each of us "veto power"[10] over inconvenient reasoning. In the tradition of PC, we will, naturally, limit these advantages to one side of the argument.

YOU CAN'T BE TOO PARTICULAR

Particular, it seems, is contagious, its letters infesting dictionary pages with illogic like fleas infesting rats with plague. Again, the word *particular* suggests that when it comes to taking offense some groups are more *particular* than others—and some are not *particular* at all. Wikipedia also focuses on the word *particular:* "Political Correctness . . . is used to describe language, policies, or measures that are intended to avoid offense or disadvantage to members of *particular* groups in society" (emphasis added).

To understand the word *particular,* consider a particularly deplorable sentence of my own making: "The rich make little effort to understand the poor, and the poor make little effort to understand anything." Whether true or not, the words are certainly not politically correct. Why? The statement stereotypes and defames a *particular* group of people.

Which group qualifies as *particular*? The rich, the poor, or the human race? Minority status is obviously not enough, for under PC some minorities are more equal than others. Consider, for instance, an eleven-million-member minority in our country that is continually demeaned and never included with the *particular* in any dictionary definition of PC. Members of this minority are routinely disparaged for their greed. Their children are routinely bullied by journalists as "privileged." What in particular is their most unforgivable sin? Success. Such success disqualifies them from any claim to be *particular*. Instead it is always fashionable for the envious to steal away their humanity forgetting that they have hearts, dreams, and loved ones. Thus dehumanized, they are perceived as legitimate hate-speech magnets. The name of the minority?

Millionaires.

In the games of politics, economics, and social status there are winners and losers. In the case of dictionary definitions, when it comes to groups qualifying as *particular*, winners need not apply. Only losers are welcome, preferably losers riding on the coattails of their loser ancestors. The more generations of losers boasted by a group's pedigree, the greater its chance at qualifying as *particular*. If a group has failed to live up to its lineage, and has achieved success, its particularity is lost.

A second way for a group to be counted as *particular* is for the group to be digitally vocal, adept at filling cyberspace and other media with complaints of injustice and victimization. To be really *particular*, the group needs to take the initiative to take offense, for there is no more *particular* and precious way to censor the arguments of rivals than to take offense. Those who have dared to become successful and have left the group are now perceived to have gone over to the light side.

Yet another sign of being *particular* is that the group has learned to hide behind its name for the purpose of not having to defend arguments or misdeeds. Imagine, for instance, we are speaking about an imaginary group known as the "Moonies." PC would tell us that demeaning Moonies is dangerous because we might ultimately dehumanize them, open the door to lunar genocide, and eliminate from the nighttime sky the Man in the Moon. Meantime, however slight the possibility of genocide, the Man in the Moon hides behind his Moonie status to excuse his ridiculous claim of being made of green cheese. However dark Mr. Moon's dark side, however persistent his lying about green cheese, we still cannot berate him. He is, after all, a member of a *particular* group.

Particularity aside, the definitions of PC typically refer not to the defamation of individuals but to the sensibilities of "groups." And we all know how sensible groups are! PC is collective thought demanding we not stereotype groups for their collective thought.

DEPLORABLE PC

Dictionaries sieve definitions out of group agreement voting in the use of words. The deplorable need not agree. Outside of dictionaries, there are any number of ways we could define PC. For its defenders, PC is the road to a New World Order free from poverty, global warming, and Republicans. If you give a man a fish, you feed him for a day, but if you forbid all words against stealing fish, the fishermen will have to feed him for a lifetime.

LAUGHING AT POLITICAL CORRECTNESS

Defenders of PC are welcome simply to dismiss the definitions that follow, as well as the rest of this book, as deplorable. Who wants to waste energy consciously rethinking habitual thought? With luck, the politically correct can even get the book condemned as inflammatory—meaning it ignites the passions of political rivals.

For the rest of us, those who imagine PC is the New Puritans' attempt to change the scarlet letter from **A** to **D**, the better to brand the pride of the deplorables, I offer my own twenty-one definition salute to PC:

1. Limiting language to achieve what limited abilities cannot.
2. The language game in which only the blind don't have to play dumb.
3. The hate speech to end all hate speech.
4. The best proof that free speech cannot travel through a mental vacuum.
5. Judging injustice by the color of its skin.
6. A verbal handicap balancing the race between races.
7. Political suppression masquerading as morality.
8. Promoting group rights at the expense of human rights.
9. Celebrating diversity of appearance over diversity of thought.
10. Freedom of boycott replacing freedom of speech.
11. An algebra in which only one side of the equation deserves equality.

12. Building private thought on the bedrock of public opinion.
13. Secular grammar editing the soul from the human spirit.
14. The bullying *of* groups edited to the bullying *by* groups.
15. Mimicking nature by moving the emptiest half of the glass to the top.
16. The new terrorism destroying livelihoods to control hearts, minds, and politics.
17. The slippery slope of progress descending toward the blind precipice of despotism.
18. Wearing the shoe of the witch hunt on the other foot.
19. The vigilantism of the New Moral Majority.
20. The r-word replacing the n-word in character assassination.
21. The oppression of language lowering socialism into communism.

These definitions sprang from my explorations of PC. I found contradictions. I found free will replaced with free excuse. I found value judgments passed off as facts. I found ideologies elevated to scripture, morality defined by the strength of political action committees. I found character assassination substituted for debate, the attack of speakers rather than their arguments, straw-man racism used to destroy reputations. I found descriptions of existence that more often ran along the fault lines of belief than cutting nature at its joints. I found a secular human spirit without a soul. I found myself borrowing all these rhetorical devices to produce the humor in this polemic—anything for a laugh.

If readers were to devote a few minutes of reflection to each of these twenty-one definitions, they could skip the rest of the chapters. But who would want to? Even Molotov himself would relish the explosion of this deplorable cocktail—the illogic of PC on the rocks with a twist of laughter.

Sip it. Savor it. Just don't blame me if you chip a tooth chewing the ice.

CHAPTER 4

HANSEL AND GRETEL'S FAVORITE WITCH RECIPES

> Then Gretel gave her a push that drove her far into it,
> and shut the iron door and fastened the bolt. Oh! then
> she began to howl quite horribly, but Gretel ran away,
> and the godless witch was miserably burnt to death.
>
> —*The Brothers Grimm*

Political correctness (PC) is the legacy of Adolf Hitler. The arguments behind PC all converge back to Hitler. Hitler told stories about the German people being superior to the rest of the world. Hitler told stories about minorities being inferior to the rest of Germans. Hitler then committed atrocities against minorities and the rest of the world. If Hitler had not been allowed to tell stories, the politically correct story goes, then he could not have committed atrocities. The stories, not the atrocities, were the problem. It is best, therefore, to cut off the tongue and fingers of all those telling or writing stories about superiority or inferiority of majorities or minorities—except, perhaps, stories that the politically correct are superior to the deplorable and proud.

Whether this Hitler logic is sound or noise, the argument is not without support and has become ever more popular with the parishioners of the New Moral Majority (NMM), who are apparently edging ever closer to becoming what they fight. As Friedrich Nietzsche warned, "He who fights with monsters should look to it that he himself does not become a monster. And if you gaze long into the abyss, the abyss also gazes into you."[1]

The fall of PC into the abyss of hate could be argued by exploring the article "Dangerous Speech and Dangerous Ideology: An Integrated Model for Monitoring and Prevention."[2] The authors, Jonathan Leader Maynard from Oxford and Susan Benesch from Harvard, explore the nature of hearing and speech needed to invoke violence (or at least destroy reputations and livelihoods).

Maynard and Benesch reason that pitting "us" against "them" (progressives against conservatives)[3] proves useful for "propaganda campaigns that depict the targeted community as . . . [an] economic threat or as inferior [deplorable, perhaps] in order to justify action against the community." Being a speaker with "authority" (Madonna? Bill Moyers?) would also prove useful for mobilizing action. An audience with "fears," "long term grievances," and "memories of historical injustice" (descendants of slaves?) is the easiest to incite to violence. Also, a "community or audience [that] relies predominantly on one source of news" (the liberal media, all editing the same stories from the same liberal perspective?) is also easy to provoke. The audience targeted to receive the violence is "dehumanized" (called racists, sexists, or xenophobes?). They are accused of being "guilty of heinous past crimes" (greedy capitalists stealing the labor of workers?). They are painted as contributing "serious and often mortal threats" (taking away funds for abortions and other "standard health care"). "Virtuetalk" is used to accuse the targeted group of "a lack of character traits, a *deplorable* [emphasis added] 'weakness,' or a range of other deficiencies" (greed, a lack of empathy for minorities, et cetera?).

Need language incite violence? What would you expect from Oxford and Harvard scholars? Wisdom? A deplorable author with no respect for PC could apply the reflections of Maynard and Benesch to suggest that the violence after Trump's election and the shooting of U.S. Congressman Steve Scalise[4] had been engineered by PC. The politically correct could retort by quoting the words of our Oxford friend Timothy Garton Ash, "It is difficult . . . to establish a firm causal connection between hateful speech and specific acts of violence—that is between something said and something done."[5] Ash's "hateful speech," of course, is not to be confused with truly politically incorrect "hate speech." To qualify as true hate speech the words must flow against the rhetoric in a one-way ideology. True hate speech is always responsible for violence—even when the violence is against the speaker. Like hate, is violence only violence when it flows against the wrong ideology?

It is true that we can use words to dehumanize our enemies and that "Gook" once helped justify Hiroshima and Nagasaki and "racist" now justifies ruining the livelihood of political opponents. It is also true, however, that once Italians were Wops and Irish were Micks. My father, when he was in the Navy during the 1920s, 30s, and 40s, thought nothing of using such terms when bantering with his multi-heritaged buddies aboard ship. Being "poor white trash" himself, I doubt that he took the labels too seriously. Despite my father's naughty words, the groups somehow avoided genocide to become assimilated into our country.

In the same way, I have been assimilated into Atlanta, being no longer dehumanized as a "Yankee." When I got to the South in 1980, I talked funny. People repeatedly asked if I was a Yankee. To avoid the prejudice, not to mention averting genocide, I learned quickly. The best way to defuse the animosity was to explain that I was from *Southern* California. Now things have changed. I just share, "I'm fixin' to carry Momma to the store," and I'm good to go anywhere in the South. Luckily for me, once you get a few miles outside Atlanta proper, it is still more correct to be politically incorrect than it is to be a Yankee. So long as there is free speech, stories may outlive the effects of governmental violence if not the ravages of PC.

Another method of comparing the relationship between words and violence is to consider the writing of Professor R. J. Rummel, the author of *Death by Government*.[6] Rummel noted that "governments have proved the most robust killing machines in history, having murdered 169,198,000 of their own citizens in the twentieth century alone." He speculates, "The more power a government has, the more it can act arbitrarily according to the whims of the elite, and the more it will make war on others and murder its foreign and domestic subjects." Such behavior, according to Rummel, is mainly true of totalitarian regimes—which, by the way, are universally acknowledged for their rigid standards of PC. Were the atrocities the result of what Hitler, Stalin, and Mao said, or was the problem in their unhesitating use of violence to silence opponents? Was free speech or its suspension the cause of the rampant murder?

LAUGHING AT POLITICAL CORRECTNESS

Beside the above speculations, the most basic argument for words being responsible for actions is that listeners do not have free will. They have only free excuse. They are not responsible (or liable) for their own actions. They can no more avoid taking offense than a kleptomaniac can avoid taking a watch. The road rage is in the road, not the driver. We are merely ping-pong balls batted hither and yon in a match between environments and genomes. We cannot help but intimidate others with violence or the threat of violence whenever we are struck with words. We are genetically incapable of being more skeptical of violence than we are of words.

PC is, nevertheless, Hitler's legacy. Hitler used the state propaganda machine to malign one of the most industrious groups in the nation, many of whom were prospering, or at least getting by, despite the dismal state of the economy ripped by war, inflation, and depression. The Nazis played on the public's envy to dehumanize this hardworking group, accusing them of "greed," of pigging up, as it were, all the money (which is ironic, considering the group's aversion to pork).

The whole affair sounds not unlike like today's PC condemning "greedy" CEOs as if the size of their salaries is to blame for others failing to develop the skills needed to demand higher incomes. The Nazis continued their propaganda campaign until it was all right to seize the property of the more successful. Hitler's attack of the able cost him many of his best scientists. Without Hitler's self-defeating racism there may have been no Hiroshima or Nagasaki but instead a charbroiled London or New York.

Hitler, of course, was not alone in using an appeal of envy to kill millions. Stalin played on envy to rack up forty-two million murders, while Mao used envy to accrue a tally of thirty-eight million. Even though Stalin and Mao each murdered twice as many of their own citizens as Hitler, neither of them committed the most unpardonable offense ever preserved by history—losing. Thus, we seldom compare our political opponents to Stalin or Mao despite the greater magnitude of the two dictators' sins; Hitler remains the bogeyman.

The name *Hitler* has been reduced to a political cliché. Whenever we lack a decent political argument, we compare our opponents to Hitler, allowing emotion to triumph over rationality. The politically correct, for instance, are forever comparing President Trump to Hitler. The revulsion we feel toward Hitler is understandable and warranted. Besides his maniacal attempt to remove an entire race from the world just because of their religion, Hitler demanded of his followers unquestioned PC. Under the Fuehrer, political incorrectness meant death. In America today, we've only gotten as far as loss of income and reputation.

Not only did Hitler demand PC, he was, at heart, a progressive. In the words of the journalist, biographer, and novelist A. N. Wilson:

> Hitler's zest for the modern, his belief that humanity would become more reasonable when it had cast off the shackles of the past—olde-tyme handwriting, religion, and so forth—and embraced science and modern roads, was a belief shared with almost all forward-thinking people at the time, and it continues to be the underlying belief-system of the liberal intelligentsia who control the West. His belief led directly to genocide and

devastating war. At the same time, he believed himself to be enlightened and forward-looking, non-smoking, vegetarian, opposed to hunting, in favour of abortion and euthanasia.[7]

Many of those who demand PC today would love nothing more than to have Hitler's power so they could kill "hate." Luckily, such New Moral Majority zealots do not have the Fuehrer's power. Not yet. PC must still contend with us deplorable and proud. Still, Hitler's legacy is not dead. In the 1950s Senator Joseph McCarthy led a witch hunt against Communists. Today, the witch hunt is on for those professing such ideological beliefs as racism, sexism, nativism, homophobia, xenophobia, intolerance, or conservativism. The destruction of reputations is already greasing the basket of deplorables. Only our deplorable pride stands between us and the total dehumanization required to slip us into the oven as outlined in that enduring German classic *Hansel and Gretel's Favorite Witch Recipes*.

CHAPTER 5

SACRED POLITICS:
THE NEW MORAL MAJORITY

To err is human, but it feels divine.

—*Mae West*

PC is the creed of the New Moral Majority (NMM) promising us the whole true truth and nothing but the true truth, so help us Nature. But since Nature never holds still, what is truth? Once it was absolute. Today truth rests in the sum of the viewpoints—of the blind. Consider, for instance, a politically correct version of an old Asian tale about a bull elephant discovered by four blind persons: an Asian American feminist, an African American communist, a European American philosopher, and a cross-undressing pole dancer.

The feminist twisted the elephant's ear and, because he trumpeted, reasoned that the elephant was a sexist who couldn't see that turnaround was fair play, not bullying. The communist slapped the creature's side and reasoned the elephant was a factory wall built by a racist capitalist who exploited minorities and supported political action committees against gay marriage or raising the minimum wage. The European American philosopher examined both the elephant's ear and side and argued that the elephant violated the law of non-contradiction—it could not possibly be both a factory wall and a sexist. And the pole dancer got trampled to death.

MORALITY OF THE MAJORITY

History repeats itself. If you've seen one moral majority, you've seen them all. Just as Jimmy Swaggart warned against the evils of sex, Hillary Clinton warns against the evils of lying. When Donald Trump won the election, the NMM all threatened to move to Canada. Oddly, none mentioned moving to Mexico. The keystone of moral majorities, even the new one, remains hypocrisy.

RELATIVE MORALITY

There are, of course, as many ways to cut the pie of morality as there are moral philosophers. Consider, for instance, morality as groupthink, morality being relative to what the majority of people have believed during the majority of history—slavery being just fine; or morality being comprised of the values voted, in the here and now, most likely to succeed—like raising a family before deciding to marry.

Often relative morality rests on reason, not groupthink. According to the Greeks, our ability to reason separates us from the beasts—but certainly not from each other. The discovery of truth rests on reason. The word *reason*, however, confuses two very different activities: (1) action reason and (2) rhetorical reason. Action reason is used to get us from point A to point B in the physical or moral world. If we are trapped in a maze and a right turn leads to a dead end, then reason dictates that a left turn may allow escape. In the hands of science, action reason has given us longer lifespans, space travel, and the digital world. The success of action reason is used to sell a very distant cousin as an identical twin: rhetorical reason.

Rhetorical reason is used to sell ideas. The philosopher Paul Feyerabend has described such reasoning as "brainwashing by argument."[1] To be considered reasonable, the parts of the sales pitch must all agree. If Tom is taller than Fred, then Fred must be shorter than Tom. If all men are mortal, and Tom and Fred are men, then Tom and Fred will eventually die. The problem with rhetorical reasoning? Future discoveries may reveal that Tom was wearing platform shoes and Fred is a cross-dresser—and not a man at all. Future discoveries too often turn today's facts into tomorrow's fairytales and the soundest rhetorical reason into noise. That rhetorical reason sells an idea tells us more about sales than truth. It doesn't matter if the pieces of a jigsaw puzzle fit together; the puzzle picture may remain fantasy, if not downright pornography.

Rhetorical reasoning is also the universal solvent, dissolving all arguments and observations at odds with passion. All moral arguments supported by rhetorical reason must be taken on faith in rhetorical reason—including the present argument. If rhetorical reasoning is our passion, then we will come up with rhetorical reasons to sell that passion. True morality gets reduced to the rhetorical reason that won the popular vote on truth.

ABSOLUTE MORALITY

A second way to view morality is to prefer God to groupthink. In such an absolute system, only a Being with an omniscient outside viewpoint can see the true Truth. Most of us call this Being God. We have faith that God wrote the Ten Commandments so we may survive our relative blindness, at least until we can see to love one another as God loves us.

UNCONTESTABLE MORALITY

The NMM does not claim its groupthink is absolute, merely uncontestable—and to contest the uncontestable is to be a villain. The uncontestable truth is reasoned to come from Mother Nature, who wrote the rules and then, in her natural wisdom, buried them. In such thinking, the uncontestable truth has always been there but only our current culture's remarkable enlightenment provides the shovels needed to dig up the uncontestable truths and bury the false ones. It is, for instance, uncontestable that sodomy is productive but capitalism is not.

In the old morality, we were commanded not to steal, with no provision being made for stealing from the rich and giving to the poor—that's found in *Robin Hood* and *Das Kapital*, not the Bible. What Jesus actually said was, "If thou wilt be perfect, go and sell that thou hast, and give to the poor, and thou shalt have treasure in heaven: and come and follow me." He didn't say anything about selling what your neighbor has and redistributing it to the poor. Providing government with the strength to abolish property rights and steal our way into Utopia comes from Marx, not Jesus.

THE ORIGINAL SEVEN DEADLY SINS

What is sin? Once, folks knew that God was good, and that good was all that stood between us and the abyss of desire. To sin was to lose sight of the Good and tumble headlong into the abyss. Without the Good, the first stolen kiss or apple never ceased to linger and beckon from the heart of chaos.

The old moral majority believed that we were created with free will, that we made choices, and that good choices ultimately had good consequences; bad choices ultimately had bad consequences. They imagined that we reaped what we had sown, if not immediately, then eventually.

In those days, sin consisted of turning away from God long enough to allow our desires to overcome our free will. Such lapses included pride, covetousness, lust, anger, gluttony, envy, sloth. Today the NMM view these "sins" as curiosities left over from a now defunct religion. Secularism is all that matters, and politically correct fashion discourages us from mentioning these curiosities in public, but since the deplorable and proud care for neither PC nor fashion, here goes:

PRIDE

Pride is the notion that we know as much as God and have every right to preheat the brimstone lest eternity not be long enough for God to achieve justice. It takes a bit of pride, for instance, to kill people in the name of Jesus. Pride, one could imagine, is the delusion that when it comes to dealing out vengeance we are playing with full decks.

GREED

Greed is a lot like covetousness, only easier to spell. Still, God tells us, "Thou shalt not covet thy neighbour's house, thou shalt not covet thy neighbour's wife, nor his manservant, nor his maidservant, nor his ox, nor his ass, nor any thing that is thy neighbour's." Nor does God say that it's okay to redistribute our neighbor's ass to those who are most likely to vote for us in the next election.

LUST

The wages of this sin, at least of the heterosexual variety, are children, whether convenient or not. In times past, the life expectancy of inconvenient children was not high. It still isn't.[2] Morality is just common sense. The inheritance of illegitimate children is far from certain, yet since lust has passed from a sin to an inalienable right, 40 percent of children now being born are, to borrow a term from English civil and canon law, *bastards,* with all the implied trimmings of disadvantage. Leaving a child, allegedly, with a distant prospect of global pollution is hardly as bad as leaving a child with an immediate lack of birthright. Nothing quite like illegitimacy allows the sins of the parents to be visited upon the children; generations are often required for bastards and their children to catch back up as they repay the debt for their parents' irresponsibility.

Lust has other liabilities. Luckily, since my hormones fell out, lust is no longer my favorite deadly sin. I now prefer gluttony.

GLUTTONY

For the politically correct, gluttony is no longer a sin but a disease. We are not obese. Our bones are "air-adverse," faltering at the approach of thin air, inviting the generation of flesh to insulate our marrow from space. For the NMM, gluttony is now a virtue. Once equality is reached, those who rule the politically correct will be able to have our cake and eat it too.

ANGER

Anger is much less fun than lust, gluttony, or covetousness. It is perhaps the least enjoyable of the seven deadly sins. But then we are all angry about PC, or we would not be reading this book. Anger has its uses.

ENVY

Lack of possession is nine-tenths of envy. Those with the most to say about greed are the envious. Envy and greed are but two sides of the same deadly sin. Greed is excessive love for what we have; envy, excessive love for what others have.

SLOTH

Sloth may be defined as not answering the door when opportunity knocks. PC ignores the sloth and legislates larger door knockers. In PC, slothful thinking is what's needed when wishful thinking doesn't work because there is no one left to tax.

THE NEW SEVEN DEADLIES

Having reviewed the seven deadlies of the old moral majority, we turn to the seven deadlies of the NMM. Gone are the good old days in which a sin was a sin, not a mistake, not a disease, not a relic of a bygone religion. Thus to the NMM, sins are not about overcoming urges but about refusing to accept ideologies, especially those masquerading as morality. To earn your secular salvation, you must simply *believe*!

Orthodoxy is rewarded, heresy penalized. The new inquisition forgoes the flames and the stake in favor of assassinating the character of the deplorable. The following heresies comprise the new seven deadlies: racism, sexism, nativism, homophobia, xenophobia, intolerance, and conservative hate speech. The details of most of these we will visit in other chapters, but before moving on we will briefly review just one—as an appetizer for what may, or may not, follow.

HOMOPHOBIA[3]

Homophobia—why be afraid? Ask Chick-fil-A president Dan Cathy. He confessed to supporting "the traditional family" and Emory and Duke universities, those bastions of academic (but nobody else's) liberty, replaced freedom of speech with freedom of boycott.[4] In the true politically correct tradition, both schools kicked Chick-fil-A off campus. The whole affair reminds me of the Pilgrims, who came to America for freedom of religion and then hung Quakers. The LGBTQ community marched in America for freedom of self-expression and then boycotted Dan Cathy for expressing himself. In America, we may not have freedom of speech, but at least we have freedom of hypocrisy.

Lest this polemic be banned from the shelves of better college bookstores, let me abstain from praising traditional marriages, although I've certainly enjoyed all three of my own. If truth be told, when I was a teenager if wearing a skirt had provided the key to the girls' shower room, I would have swapped genders quicker than Hillary Clinton swapped residences to run for the Senate. If a man wants to marry his brother and father, don't brag about it to me. While year after year, decade after decade, century after century, fornication tops the sexual bell curve, incest, homosexuality, and polygamy never fall completely off the curve. The distance of sexual perversion from the mean matters less than the strength of the political action committee.

Do I believe in same-sex marriage? Yes. There is little doubt that according to the passions of today's court system same-sex marriage legally occurs. Do I believe that same-sex marriage is the way to "be fruitful, and multiply, and replenish the earth"? No. Like the spark from two stones, the collision may conceive a fire more readily than a child. Still, every lightning bolt has a golden lining: if the lesbian and gay community is successful in their membership drive, we will no longer need to waste our tax dollars on teaching birth control in kindergarten.

As Mark Twain wrote in an unsent letter, "We are ruled by a King just as other absolute monarchies are. His name is The Majority. He is mighty in bulk and strength…. He rules by the right of possessing less money and less brains and more ignorance than the other competitor for the throne." There is a certain comfort to be found—not!—having the NMM holding us at bay with the threat of public opinion. The n-word is out; the f-word, in. Discrimination[5] is out; color-blindness, in.[6] Who knows when a Newer Moral Majority will vote a new, uncontestable, seven deadly sins most likely to succeed?

CHAPTER 6

SLEEPING WITH BILL COSBY— THE ROUTINE THAT ENDED POLITICAL CORRECTNESS

You are aware that public men get ample credit for all the sins they commit, and for a multitude of other sins they were never guilty of.

—*Mark Twain*

So, which are you? A sexist or a racist? Either way, you fail the PC taste test. You may have no taste at all—thanks to the paradoxical case of Bill Cosby.

What, we may ask, did Bill Cosby do to me? Did he slip me a Mickey Finn? Did he tarnish my virtue? With no need for solid proof, oh, the stories I could invent—the stories most anyone could invent. But since, I'm capitalizing on Cosby's name by borrowing it in the title of a chapter, I'll make no claims.

In America, as we will see, a man is innocent until more-or-less proven guilty in a court of law, unless, perhaps, he is politically incorrect. Then the moral vigilantes dispense with the law, lynch reputations, and remove any need for a trial before dragging the man's name through the mud. Grant accusation the authority of conviction and let the witch hunts begin, as every grudge and regret from the past half century is dredged wily nilly from a well of imagination and memory without a drop of responsibility. Unchecked by a need for proof, the accusations can morph into mass hysteria, much as when during the Inquisition old women were accused of witchcraft in order to seize their property.[1]

There are high courts and low courts, but the lowest court of all is the court public opinion. It's verdicts are too often the same: "Crucify him!" Despite the thinking of PC, trial by jury still has its advantages, unless we enjoy tyranny.

Bill Cosby himself doesn't lynch reputations; he hangs juries. Little wonder. To love Bill Cosby is to qualify as a sexist. To hate Bill Cosby is to qualify as a racist. It is only fitting that Cosby came in, and went out, making us laugh at our shortcomings as human beings. To know of him is to be politically incorrect.

My first contact with Bill Cosby's comedy came in 1966. I was fourteen years old. That was the year that Cosby recorded his "Chicken Heart" routine. At a friend's, I listened to the cut one time. Fifty years later the "bump bump ... bump bump" and an image of a little boy smearing Jell-O on the floor remain a part of the flotsam and jetsam of my mind.

Bill Cosby made me laugh. Like the talent of so many other gifted entertainers, Cosby has made life, in my own estimation, a better place in which to spend my days. In the half century since his *Wonderfulness* album was released, Cosby acted in *I Spy* to break the racial barrier on TV, won Emmy's, and produced and stared on *The Cosby Show,* which was the number one show in America from 1985 to 1989. Bill Cosby also showed his respect for learning, earning a PhD from Temple University and receiving almost as many honorary degrees as President John Kennedy had adulteries (well, maybe not that many). His talent has allowed him to amass a fortune of four hundred million dollars.[2]

JUMPING AT OPPORTUNITY

According to the stories told about him, Bill is a prime example of my maxim, "The primary cause of sin is opportunity; gluttony thrives on smorgasbords, not famines." The maxim is, of course, false. Sin has nothing to do with opportunity. Sin comes from within, not without. The lust for forbidden fruit—whether for flesh or vengeance—is still sin whether or not the fruit is in reach. Opportunity just makes it easier to reveal our hearts. Sadly, I would think, Bill Cosby had more opportunity to reveal his heart than most of us blessed with inopportunity can imagine. If the news stories are to be believed, Cosby sinned both inside and outside his heart. Eternity may not recognize the boundary between heart and world, but Bill Cosby's alleged crimes, though in no way legal, were in the words of politically correct immigration jargon, "undocumented."

Bill's greatest crime may not have been his supposed violation of the basic human right to say no to personal contact. It may not have even been the allure of his fame, wealth, and charisma or the attraction of taking down someone whose talent has placed him at the top of the game. Bill's greatest crime may have been his violation of PC.

In Washington, D.C. in 2004, on the fiftieth anniversary of the U.S. Supreme Court's decision on *Brown v. Board of*

Education, Bill Cosby addressed three thousand of the black elite and failed miserably at PC:

> Today, ladies and gentlemen, in our cities and public schools we have fifty percent drop out. In our own neighborhood, we have men in prison. No longer is a person embarrassed because they're pregnant without a husband. (clapping) No longer is a boy considered an embarrassment if he tries to run away from being the father of the unmarried child (clapping).... Are you not paying attention, people with their hat on backwards, pants down around the crack. Isn't that a sign of something, or are you waiting for Jesus to pull his pants up (laughter and clapping).[3]

Three weeks later in Chicago, at the annual convention of Jesse Jackson's Rainbow/PUSH Coalition, Bill Cosby went on to say, "Let me tell you something. Your dirty laundry gets out of school at 2:30 every day. It's cursing and calling each other nigger as they walk up and down the street. They think they're hip. They can't read; they can't write. They're laughing and giggling and they're going nowhere."[4]

Being accused of ignoring that white racism was the real source of the problem, Bill Cosby spoke of the "analgesia" that accompanies centering on victimization and said, "It keeps a person frozen in their seat. It keeps you frozen in the hole you are sitting."[5] It was almost as if Bill Cosby believed that hanging on to our injustices does not free our hands to build a new future. He joined another famous African American who was more interested in his fellows getting on than getting even—Booker T. Washington:

There is another class of coloured people who make a business of keeping the troubles, the wrongs, and the hardships of the Negro race before the public. Having learned that they are able to make a living out of their troubles, they have grown into the settled habit of advertising their wrongs—partly because they want sympathy and partly because it pays. Some of these people do not want the Negro to lose his grievances, because they do not want to lose their jobs.[6]

Like Cosby, Washington thought the way out was education and success, not playing the victim. Whatever his similarities to the former slave, Bill Cosby received a standing ovation in Washington and "thunderous applause" in Chicago. But, unlike Washington, Cosby lived in the age of political correctness, not the age of slavery and Jim Crow. The politically correct are not as forgiving.

What was the eventual cost of Bill Cosby's political incorrectness? What was his reward for admitting that African Americans were not stereotypes but real live flesh and blood humans, who, like the rest of us, as Mark Twain noted, sometimes need to blush? The applause didn't last. The damage had already been done.

PRESUMED GUILTY

It has often been said about the arts, "You can make a killing, but you can't make a living." Comedian Hannibal Buress is one of those few who are talented enough to be making a killing. According to the website Celebrity Net Worth, he's accumulated a two-million-dollar fortune. Like

Cosby, he's part of the only minority in America that it's still perfectly acceptable to demean: millionaires.

In 2014, Buress performed a stand-up comedy routine that spoke to Cosby's political incorrectness. The routine included the lines, "Bill Cosby has the fuckin' smuggest old black man public persona that I hate. He gets on TV, 'Pull your pants up black people, I was on TV in the 80s! I can talk down to you because I had a successful sitcom!' Yeah, but you rape women, Bill Cosby, so turn the crazy down a couple of notches."[7] While Cosby had used the politically incorrect n-word, Buress confined himself to the now politically correct f-word. Nor was Buress content with getting a laugh out of obscenity and sensationalism. He was careful to invite his audience to google "Bill Cosby rape" when they got home, lest Buress's two-hundred-times-more-successful, politically incorrect rival go unpunished for his sins.

The point here is not whether Bill Cosby is guilty or innocent—that we will leave up to trial by jury, not vigilantism. The point is that, up until Bill Cosby violated PC, his fame had shielded him from the brunt of accusations and had shielded his accusers from giving in to any lust for vengeance clouding their hearts. Will Hannibal Buress similarly reap what he sowed? His attack against Bill Cosby has certainly not, as yet, hurt his own career. In 2016, he appeared in two computer-animated box-office hits that together grossed a billion dollars: *The Angry Bird Movie* and *The Secret Life of Pets*. Buress may never see his own two million dollars grow to Cosby's four hundred million, but he may nevertheless be remembered as the comedian who took down the most beloved African American TV star of the twentieth century, the icon who was for many otherwise culturally segregated white Americans the only black face that they either knew or loved.

In the PC tradition, while Bill Cosby was still legally innocent, having not been convicted of any crime, he was stripped of his television contracts, his agent, even many of his honorary degrees. His alleged abuses of human rights were judged to outweigh his contributions to his race and to stand above his talent, his ability, and his success.

How will history view Bill Cosby? It's hard to say. Alexander the Great conquered the world before his death at thirty-two. Even though his empire was diced by his generals shortly after his death, he—being a student of Aristotle—nevertheless spread Greek culture throughout the world, playing his part in disseminating the philosophies that would blossom into the scientific revolution two millennia later. As mentioned in our first chapter, Washington and Jefferson, up until now at least, were remembered for founding a great nation rather than their peccadillos. But then they didn't have to contend with the NMM.

Alexander, of course, was politically correct because he controlled the politics of his day and it was not only politically incorrect but lethal to argue with him. Washington and Jefferson—if you asked the British—were as politically incorrect as incorrect can be. Today, however, PC allows us to strip Alexander, Washington, and Jefferson of their greatness. Even though it is fallacious to say so, their records on human rights were deplorable, making Bill Cosby in comparison, whether he is innocent or guilty, look like a saint.

If Bill Cosby had never existed, would the world be a better place? If Bill Cosby's accusers had never existed, would the world be a better place? If you and I had never existed, would the world be a better place? If the world had never existed, would the world be a better place? Philosophy aside, as I've already mentioned, Bill Cosby's case provides us with a dilemma. If we damn him, suggesting that putting another black man in prison will hardly rock the balance of the criminal justice system, then we are racists. If we praise him—as if Bill Cosby's contributions outweighed his alleged victimization of women—we are sexists.

Damn him? Praise him? Judge him as we hoped to be judged for our own sins? Whatever our approach, the deplorable and proud, I believe, owe Bill Cosby a significant debt. By turning most who believe the news into racists or sexists, he has slain universal political correctness. "Bump bump … bump bump … bump bump…." Let's go for the Jell-O!

CHAPTER 7

CRYING "FIRE!"

It is by the goodness of God that in our country we
have those three unspeakably precious things:
freedom of speech, freedom of conscience, and the
prudence never to practice either.

—*Mark Twain*

Let me begin with a few questions about this chapter. Which of my arguments are true? Why? Which of my arguments are false? Why? How many others would find this chapter worth their time? Based on the chapter, should I be allowed to speak on a college campus?

If you say that you cannot possibly answer the questions without reading the chapter, then you are obviously not politically correct. From my earlier confession of being "deplorable," the politically correct could safely infer that nothing in the chapter is worth reading and that no one should be allowed to read it. Freedom of speech has its limits, and I—like one crying "Fire!" to a crowded theater or an execution squad—do not fall within those limits.

With that preface, allow me to fire away at those who would deny us free speech.

The heartfelt bounce of my dog tells the story of the walk or bone, but other than being made in God's image what separates us from the animals and vegetables is our ability to tell stories that transcend immediate actions. Thus, in a free republic, our greatest and rightly most cherished gift is the gift of free speech—the right to tell or not tell our stories; the right to accept or reject the stories of others. When this right is no longer tolerated, a republic is no longer free.

In this chapter, we will explore free speech, visiting the following deplorable tales:

- Who's Afraid of Free Speech
- Book Burning in New York
- A Parable on Freedom of Silence
- Free Excuse versus Free Will and Free Speech
- *On Liberty*—John Stuart Mill Style
- A Free Republic versus the Tyranny of a False Majority
- Freedom of Boycott—Freedom of Speech

WHO'S AFRAID OF FREE SPEECH?

The power of freedom of speech is bounded by eloquence and skepticism. One without the other can create an imbalance, inviting the wiles of demagogues and fools. Shakespeare provides examples. In *Julius Caesar*, Mark Antony's eloquence captivates the crowd. In *Othello*, the Moor's failure at skepticism sacrifices his "world of kisses," Desdemona. Those who disparage free speech either fear their own lack of eloquence or others' lack of skepticism. Or they fear the discovery of truth.

Except perhaps for those hiding their real agendas, censors of free speech are elitists enamored of their own superior cleverness, insight, and perception, and/or convinced of the inferiority, weakness, and inadequacy of others. Just as we censor the world for our children until they are mature enough to scrutinize their surroundings for themselves, so the elitist, out of disdain for others' hypothetically blunted perception and thought, dons an egotistical, bloated paternalism for greater ease in censoring the world. Despite constant proclamations of our created equality, elitists fear their dearth of eloquence or our feebleness of skepticism. The deniers of free speech, therefore, fashion excuses to protect the "politically challenged" from the very stories that testify to the diversity of our humanity.

To use a largely metaphorical example, purely for the sake of argument, the cry of "Fire!" must be suppressed, the elitists claim, because the common folk lack the common sense to detect the common absence of flame, smoke, and heat, the common intelligence to judge the truth and avert the stampede. The elitists share a basic skepticism about the capacity for skepticism of those they imagine to be less savvy, cunning, and gifted than themselves. Censors, their hearts and minds aflame with arrogance, are far from cool about free speech.[1]

BOOK BURNING—NEW YORK STYLE

Which brings us to the elite of the elite, the arrogant of the arrogant. No one's ambivalence toward free speech tops that of New York publishing. When, a decade ago, O. J. Simpson's book *If I Did It* was purchased by HarperCollins there was uproar in the publishing community. I remember reading an editorial in *Publisher's Weekly* in which then Editor in Chief, Sara Nelson, declared, "This is not about being heard. This is about trying to cash in, in a pathetic way, on some notoriety." In other words, let's take no chance of enlightening the stupid mob. Whether or not O. J. wrote anything worth reading was inconsequential.[2] Fearing that not even the elitism of the New York critics could tame the mob's hunger for sensationalism, the New York elite quibbled and dribbled, overwhelmed by the reimbursement of the author, not the quality of his words.

In philosophy, this is known as *ad hominem* or "to the man" fallacy. For example, four hundred years earlier, in a more civilized age, it didn't matter that Sir Francis Bacon was a crook who committed twenty some counts of bribery, was sent to the Tower, and fined £40,000. It didn't matter that at age forty-five he had sex with a fourteen-year-old girl (if Bacon had any inclination to consummate the marriage—he got the dowry either way). Bacon nevertheless wrote a book famous for scrapping an older system of logic and replacing it with a newer one that was more congenial for concealing the fallacies routinely passed off as scientific knowledge. Readers, rather than wasting time judging Bacon's peccadillos, applauded his literary efforts. Readers still do. Unsoiled by the reputation of its author, the book stood or fell on its arguments and has stood the test of time even though Bacon did not stand the moral scrutiny of his contemporaries.

Times have changed. Now authors' political correctness (PC) is more important than what they write. At the end of 2016, Simon and Schuster, for instance, reportedly advanced Milo Yiannopoulos, an "alt-right," once-upon-a-time senior editor at Breitbart, $250,000 for an autobiography entitled *Dangerous*. Again, there was a mindless intellectual stir. One hundred and sixty people, including authors and agents, wrote letters of protest to Simon and Schuster to condemn the book that hadn't yet been written and certainly hadn't been read. Members of that bastion of a liberal culture took advantage of their freedom of speech to pooh-pooh a conservative author cashing in on his own freedom. No one was analyzing the holes in the minefield of the author's words. The author, and not his arguments, were what was important. In America, one of our inalienable rights has always been to censure the books we are too stupid, busy, or prejudiced to read. Groupthink is groupthink, requiring only the imagined superiority of the small minds.

In a "Soapbox" article in *Publisher's Weekly*, the editorial director of the august Farrar, Straus and Giroux Books for Young Readers, Joy Peskin, similarly protested. Joy was concerned that Milo shunned PC. He was the self-dubbed super villain of the Internet. He was banned from Twitter for saying naughty things about African American actress Leslie Jones, meaning he must be a racist and misogynist because no one but a hater of African Americans and women would dare discredit a member of their ranks.

Joy wrote, "I would ask my colleagues . . . to think long and hard about future publishing deals that give a mainstream platform to the so-called alt-right."[3] She also wondered if Milo's book would be published at all "if the industry was predominantly run by women of color as opposed to white men."

Joy is obviously proud of the superiority of a New York publishing industry that still controls the "mainstream platform," but I'm not sure where she dug up the research showing that women of color are against free speech and white men—such as those at Houghton Mifflin, who published *Mein Kampf*—are for it, but it doesn't really matter. It doesn't matter that Milo is gay and attacking him proves homophobia and misandry as surely as attacking a black female proves racism and misogyny. Milo is also a conservative, which evidently outweighs any PC brownie points for being an outlier on the sexual bell curve. If he were a Marxist, attacking him would be politically incorrect.

What did matter was that in an edited video on Twitter Milo denied that the age of consent was "this black and white thing" and said that relationships between "younger boys and older men . . . can be hugely positive experiences."

What was Milo thinking? This year, homophobia is a sin but pedophobia remains a moral command (from public opinion I guess; political correctness ignores biblical prescriptions, so exactly where secular values come from is sort of up in the air—until the next vote). Was Milo recalling the Oscar Wilde fiasco? Was he thinking about the beneficial effect that the older slave Jim had on young Huckleberry Finn's moral awakening? Was Milo ruminating on Francis Bacon marrying a fourteen-year-old for her dowry? Was Milo behind the times, romanticizing the mentoring program of the Greek military or considering, perhaps, how King Tut married his half-sister when she was nine? Had Milo recently been to Mississippi to attend a wedding between an older man and a fifteen-year-old boy? To what type of "relationship" was Milo referring: a mentorship, married sex, fornication, fishing to the music of a different stream? Simon and Schuster apparently didn't probe that deeply. Happy to have an excuse for pleasing the NMM, they used ad hominem logic to cancel Milo's book contract.

Hearing about the Milo fuss, my first thought was much the same as it had been when the Simpson book deal raised the ire of the New-York-publishing politically correct. Why not instead capitalize on publishing the books and burn them on the steps of the New York Public Library? The conflagration would make a sterner and more accurate statement of the depth of New York publishing's respect for and commitment to free speech. Inquisitors rooting out heresies against public opinion love fires. There is nothing more compelling than a charbroiled stake surrounded by the ashes of those challenging groupthink.

Am I being deplorable? Is free speech overrated? While bullying by individuals is detested, bullying by public opinion is encouraged; public intolerance of capitalists—even sodomitical or fornicating capitalists[4]—and other deplorables is even embraced. As previously described, we call this intolerance voted most likely to succeed PC.

For the purpose of convicting the incorrect, such correctness has replaced trial by jury. Twain was well aware of the tension between public opinion and free speech, remarking, "As an active privilege . . . [free speech] ranks with the privilege of committing murder; we may exercise it if we are willing to take the consequences." Despite the imagined enlightenment of PC, nothing has changed. Groupthink is as pitiful as always as freedom of boycott replaces freedom of speech.[5]

A PARABLE ON FREEDOM OF SILENCE

How free, how sacred is our freedom of speech? As the First Amendment promises, "Congress shall make no law . . . abridging the freedom of speech," and the Fourteenth Amendment—depending on whether the court is liberal or conservative—incorporates this no-no into state legislatures as well, but not necessarily into PC, which is still free to abridge any rights it so chooses.

One could imagine that if we really had freedom of speech, then we would have the freedom to speak or not to speak. Indeed, Miami School of Law Associate Professor Caroline Mala Corbin has eloquently argued against compelled speech:

> The right against compelled speech is firmly established in First Amendment jurisprudence: "Freedom of thought protected by the First Amendment . . . includes both the right to speak freely and the right to refrain from speaking at all." . . . Forcing someone to speak or support a message not their own has several negative consequences. Most obviously, it offends the autonomy of the speaker, interfering with her self-realization and undermining the freedom of thought necessary for independent decision-making. Furthermore, by misrepresenting the speaker's true point of view, compelled speech distorts the marketplace of idea and democratic deliberation.[6]

Corbin supplies legal precedent after legal precedent to support her position. For our purposes, we will examine but one deplorable parable of my own making. Suppose a devout Christian owns a wedding cake shop, and a pampered fifteen-year-old boy in a three-hundred-dollar cowboy hat and eight-hundred-dollar alligator cowboy boots comes in to purchase a cake. He announces that come the end of the month he is going to marry his father and his pet sheep and wants the three of them on the cake top, father in back with his hand on the son's right shoulder, sheep in front with the son's hand on his right rump, the hope being to dramatize the affection and solidarity the three share.[7]

Now suppose that the shop owner is behind the times and that in hanging onto Christianity he is part of the Old Moral Majority rather than the new one and has these silly, outmoded theories about the inadvisability of homosexuality and bestiality and incest and ephebophilia[8] and polygamy just because their prohibition appears in some dusty old tome with the family tree inside the front cover—a tree that refuses to bend in the direction that the customer is proposing for his father, himself, and the sheep. Does the shop owner have free speech? Can he look the customer in the eye and say absolutely nothing? Can the misguided Christian community follow the teachings of Gandhi and King and sit peaceably behind the counter, perhaps with a "Silence is Golden" placard? If civil disobedience is fair for Gandhi and King, it is certainly fair for the deplorable and proud. No? Yes?

Does the shop owner have any right to plead freedom of silence and speech? Maybe so, but he still might find himself denounced as a *próvatophobe*[9] if the story goes viral. Will the cake-shop owner be boycotted by the incestuous fathers and sons running in flocks across the sheep ranches of America? Will he be sued for discrimination by those citing laws that are senior to the most senior amendment in our Bill of Rights? Do we really have a constitutional right to free speech? Can we remain silent when spoken to by those with different moral viewpoints than our own—even if others find the silence demanded by PC being in this case politically incorrect?

And what if the sheep is already married or the son has a nubile mistress or two on the side? Will throwing adultery or fornication into the mix confuse the issues? I tell you, it's enough to make your moral compass spin like a roulette wheel.

Not to worry. As the eighteenth century philosopher David Hume reasoned in his *Treatise on Human Nature*: "Reason is, and ought only to be the slave of the passions, and can never pretend to any other office than to serve and obey them."[10] If perchance Hume's statement challenges our passions, we will naturally find it unreasonable. But should the shop owner's case reach the Supreme Court, the supremacists would use the universal solvent of reason to wash away all arguments at odds with their passions for federal over states' rights—the letter of the law having the force of alphabet soup, the spirit of the law being no more than the passion of the justices. In truth, however, there would be no need for a trial because a boycott of the shop owner's bakery, organized by the brotherhood and sisterhood of the politically correct, would put him out of business without any need for a conviction—unless the deplorable and proud threw parties, purchasing enough cakes to outweigh the passions and flagging appetites of the boycotters.

FREE WILL, FREE EXCUSE, AND FREE SPEECH

But enough parables. Two of the most popular reasons for banning free speech hinge on free excuse: the "offense argument" and the "words-made-me-do-it argument."

According to the offense argument, the best defense is to take strong offense, the approach requiring no reason—only anger, tears, or the threat of PC. The offense argument is just too precious. If readers are offended by talk of homosexuality, bestiality, incest, and polygamy because these are noted as sexual perversions in the Good Book, then my writing should be banned. If readers are offended by my positioning the four biblical perversions alongside one another as if homosexuality, bestiality, incest, and polygamy were merely peas in the perversion pod—all sharing their moral justification on reasoning honed for the occasion to fit passion—then my writing should be banned. If I am offended by those who can't take a little irony and sarcasm, then any criticism offered by those protesting my writing should be banned. In other words, the word *offend* may be used to blackmail anyone into remaining silent (or not) on any subject—providing that they are not Christian owners of cake shops.

Nothing takes more of our time than *taking*. We *take* the bait, the lessons, the serve, and the suckers. We *take* possession of or a fancy to. We *take* pieces in chess and match points in tennis. We *take* hold, advice, possession, and ill. We *take* and we *take* and we give and we *take*, yet it's hard to give what others refuse to *take*. *Taking* offense is like *taking* a look; we *take* what is useful and reject what is not, see what we need and ignore what we don't. The looks we *take* give us a seeing advantage. The offenses we *take* give us a social advantage. We *take* offense as a weapon against the offender. We *take* offense no differently than we *take* a tennis serve—with every intention of returning it in kind.

The only ones with no option but to *take* offense are children. Part of becoming a grown-up is learning not to *take* offense, to let taunts pass by like curveballs outside the strike zone as we concentrate our efforts on hitting home runs. To witness those who *take* offense is to witness juveniles, not adults—they need to grow up before playing with the big boys. *Taking* offense is the favorite strategy of those afraid or incapable of *taking* action.

We and we alone are responsible for any offense we allow to linger in those private stories we call our minds. No one ever gave offense to someone who refused to *take* it. In the words of Booker T. Washington, "I would permit no man . . . to narrow and degrade my soul by making me hate him."[11] Let those who *take* offense keep it, not use it to eliminate the free speech we depend upon for our way of life. Crying about offense is a bit like crying about spilt milk when someone is about to steal and eat the cow; our attention is misplaced, our time—and everyone else's—is wasted.

A second favorite argument using free excuse to dismiss freedom of speech (and freedom of silence) revolves around the excuse that "the words made me do it." Violence is caused by words. Our chapter "Hansel and Gretel's Favorite Witch Recipes" discussed possible relationships between the words of PC and liberal love destroying property and maiming or attempting to kill U.S. congressmen. A much more thorough treatment of free speech and violence appears in Oxford Professor Timothy Garton Ash's *Free Speech*,[12] including court rulings on requirements for convicting a speaker of inciting violence. Read it if you are interested.

The politically correct love to use the words-cause-violence argument to justify inciting silence among white supremacists. Patrick Henry said, "Give me liberty or give me death!" PC edits the sentiment to read, "Give us silence or we'll kill your livelihood." The question remains, which group does more to build the name recognition of violence, the white supremacists or the press? In the words of Mark Twain, "There are laws to protect the freedom of the press's speech, but none that are worth anything to protect the people from the press."

I subscribe to the *New York Review of Books*, a liberal look at the arts. For months before the last presidential election, the name *Trump*, and often a caricature poking fun at his hairstyle, appeared on practically every cover. Just as the press gave President Trump the name recognition needed to win the election, so the press builds the name recognition of violence.

When it comes to recognizing violence, the evening news is a great example. We live on a planet with more than seven billion people. On a given day, how many of these people laugh, how many maim or kill their neighbors? If we analyze the evening news, how many stories are about laughter, how many about the violence of human beings or nature? When I googled "white supremacism" I got seven million results; googling "food drives" gave me twenty-one million results. Can we really imagine that the news provides us with a representative sample of love and hate groups on Planet Earth? Does reporting only the violence bring us closer to the true truth or the fake news? So long as laughter doesn't pass as news, should we regard what passes as news with laughter?

Editors and reporters are fond of blaming President Trump for their rise in awareness of white supremacism. Which would end awareness of white supremacism more quickly, impeaching President Trump or impeaching the integrity of the liberal press for giving the supremacists a name recognition unwarranted by their numbers? Similarly, if in America ten million identify themselves as LGBT and there are 10.7 million millionaires,[13] and both groups are comprised of human beings, so both have every reason to blush, why does the press report the blushing of only one group? As much as I hate the bias of the evening news, I value the freedom of the press more. Protecting all other freedoms, our freedom of speech—even the press's creatively biased version—comes first, ranking up there with our freedom of skepticism.

That said, PC's push to squelch free speech in order to end violence is proof of the triumph of free excuse[14] over free will. Are those who manufacture bullets and words responsible for the violence of idiots who have loaded the projectiles into their guns and minds? I think not. The wrong speech strikes our eardrums to wade through our neural streams and convulse us with pure stimulus-response violence—or so the story goes. The story, of course, is neuro-astrology, a tale told to ban free speech.

Run an experiment for yourself. Look directly before you at the book or screen. What do you see? Now instead open up your peripheral vision. While continuing to point your eyes in the direction of the print, be aware of how much space or air there is between your nose and the words. Be aware of how far the book or screen is in front of the wall or floor.

Your perception of the world does not depend on the light waves striking the back of your eyes. It depends on what *you* do with the information. The same is true with the sound waves striking your ear drums. What you do with the information depends on *you*. We are not controlled by the sound waves and light waves instigated by words. We make choices, and we are responsible for the choices we make.

As mentioned, the balance between eloquence and skepticism determines the benefits or danger of free speech. In the case of violence, it is the job of skepticism to outweigh the power of eloquence. Jeffrey Dahmer and Alexander the Great were both serial killers. Both died young—reaping what they had sown. Alexander's fierce superiority at organized homicide dwarfed Dahmer's taste for death, yet Alexander is remembered as the man who conquered the world; Dahmer, as a monster. Such is the power of words to justify actions.

We call a serial killer on a battlefield a "hero."[15] We call a serial killer operating an electric chair an "executioner." We call a serial killer operating a manual vacuum aspirator an "advocate for women's rights." The words justify the homicides only if they are believed. A father feels no better that his beloved daughter is killed by an "executioner"; a mother, no better if her beloved son is killed by a hero; a grandparent, no better to learn that a grandchild's development was terminated by a licensed physician. The father, mother, and grandparent have a right to be skeptical about justification of actions by words even though the executioner, hero, and physician were not.

The only way I can balance my passion for life and property with my passion for freedom of speech is to imagine that not even the greatest words can justify the worst actions or that banning words can banish actions. Banning talk of racism will end racism no sooner than banning talk of war will end war—although a little more skepticism might do much to end both. I imagine responsibility for the actions I commit. Whether the word *fire* is a warning or a command, my decision to trample my neighbor in the theater[16] or pull the trigger in the execution squad is just that, a decision—a word to be skeptical of or to believe depending on my moral persuasion. I similarly imagine we are ultimately responsible for our choices and actions; there is no need to blame words. Those who wish to banish freedom of speech are those who also wish to banish free will, blaming the sound waves striking eardrums or the light waves striking eyes for our actions—as if we are not free to step back, look, listen, think, and decide.

ON LIBERTY—JOHN STUART MILL STYLE

While *offense* and *violence* are great words for quelling outbreaks of free speech (or freedom of silence), what are some famous arguments supporting free speech? John Milton, in a polemic arguing for the liberty of unlicensed printing, wrote, "Who ever knew Truth put to the worse, in a free and open encounter?"[17] Similarly, in a single paragraph of *On Liberty*, John Stuart Mill offered three free-speech rules of thumb:

> If all mankind minus one were of one opinion, mankind would be no more justified in silencing that one person than he, if he had the power, would be justified in silencing mankind.... But the peculiar evil of silencing expression of an opinion is that it is robbing the human race, posterity as well as the existing generation.... If the opinion is right, they are deprived of the opportunity of exchanging error for truth; if wrong, they lose, what is almost as great a benefit, the clearer perception and livelier impression of truth produced by its collision with error.[18]

Mill's words illuminate my cake-shop parable. First, Mills argues that whether or not the beliefs of the NMM are correct, I should not be coerced into silence about freedom of silence any more than the NMM should be coerced into silence because of my freedom.

Second, if the NMM is wrong and homosexuality, incest, bestiality, and polygamy are just the emperor's new nudity clothed by nothing but groupthink, then my parable has helped to uncover the truth. Had I been silenced about promoting our right to silence, then mankind and sheep-kind would have been robbed of exchanging error for truth.

If, however, the NMM has the truth, then my erroneous parable has given "the clearer perception and livelier impression of truth produced by its collision with error." We can now—instead of resting on "common opinion" and "everyone knows"—understand that the moral truth of a secular world is voted in by groupthink, public relations, and politics, not God, and that sodomy, incest, bestiality, and polygamy just need a few parades and a well-organized collective bargaining campaign and they too can rise to the moral top of the sexual bell curve along with fornication.

My real hope is that in daring to confront freedom of silence I have caused us to look a little harder at freedom of speech itself. Maybe I have caused us to consider that we are mixing two different questions: What is right? And what are our rights? First, is fishing to the music of a different creek morally right or morally wrong? And second, do we have a right to live our lives according to the dictates of our moral consciences (providing no one else is victimized by being forced to pay the medical expenses or child support incurred by our lifestyles)? To condemn homosexuality, fornication, incest, polygamy, or bestiality confers no right to preheat the brimstone as if eternity is too short for God to set things right. To support freedom of speech implies no respite from skepticism regarding the babble streaming from the mouths of fools. Toleration demands neither agreement nor belief.

A FREE REPUBLIC VERSUS THE TYRANNY OF A FALSE MAJORITY

Having taken PC's attack on free speech personally, it's time to view the attack's threat to our republic entire. If, as fourth President of the United States and primary author of the Constitution, James Madison, put it, if our republic is to avoid "A rage . . . for an equal division of property, or for any other improper or wicked project,"[19] then freedom of speech is paramount to the perpetuity of our republic. Allow me to explain.

Having just fought a war to escape the abuses of a central government, the American colonies were a mite wary of surrendering their rights to another central government. In their collaboration on the Federalist Papers, James Madison, Alexander Hamilton, and John Jay assumed the task of selling the federal government to the people in order to get the Constitution ratified. The sale was no easy job, because the people were nearly evenly divided and many, in Madison's words, exhibited "prevailing and increasing distrust of public engagements, and alarm for private rights, which are echoed from one end of the continent to the other." Some things, it seems, never change.

In Federalist Paper No. 9, Hamilton wrote about the instability of earlier republics:

> It is impossible to read the history of the petty republics of Greece and Italy without feeling sensations of horror and disgust at the distractions with which they were continually agitated, and at the rapid succession of revolutions by which they were kept in a state of perpetual vibration between the extremes of tyranny and anarchy.

In Federalist Paper No. 10, Madison attributed the demise of republics to what he called *factions*, "a number of citizens, whether amounting to a majority or a minority of the whole, who are united and actuated by some common impulse of passion, or of interest, adversed to the right of other citizens, or to the permanent and aggregate interests of the community."

Certainly, Madison imagined, opinions regarding religion or favorite leaders could bring about factions, but the "most common and durable source of factions has been the various and unequal distribution of property. Those who hold and those who are without property have ever formed distinct interests in society."

Madison felt that such conflicting interests were inevitable. As he put it:

> Theoretic politicians, who have patronized . . . [pure democracy] have erroneously supposed that by reducing mankind to a perfect equality in their political rights, they would, at the same time, be perfectly equalized and assimilated in their possessions, their opinions, and their passions.

In this, Madison's words support our own idea that equal rights under the law cannot make people who are unequal, equal. Madison attributed this natural inequality to inequality in "faculties," which the Oxy Morons define as, "An ability or aptitude, whether natural or acquired, for any special kind of action." In Madison's words,

> The diversity in the faculties of men, from which the rights of property[20] originate, is not less an insuperable obstacle to a uniformity of interests. *The protection of the faculties is the first object of government.* From the protection of different and unequal faculties of

acquiring property, the possession of different degrees and kinds of property immediately results; and from the influence of these on the sentiments and views of the respective proprietors, ensues a division of the society into different interests and parties. (emphasis added)

While the faction without property might argue that abolishing the liberty to acquire property would solve the problem of factions, Madison seemed to anticipate this argument, admitting, "Liberty is to faction what air is to fire.... But it could not be less folly to abolish liberty, which is essential to political life, because it nourishes faction, than it would be to wish the annihilation of air, which is essential to animal life, because it imparts to fire its destructive agency."

For Madison, a minority faction "may clog the administration, it may convulse the society; but it will be unable to execute and mask its violence" because, under the Constitution, the majority will vote against it. The problem in Madison's eyes was the majority faction, because it may "sacrifice to its ruling passion or interest both the public good and the rights of other citizens."

For a republic to endure, therefore, the key was to avoid majority factions, which Madison hoped could be accomplished by representative rather than true democratic rule,[21] the factions being diluted by a handpicked congress elected by a diverse populace representing many, many factions, none of them being strong enough to accomplish much mischief. Madison shares the exact arguments for how his Constitution would use factionalism to check factionalism, but for our purposes it is enough to note that a majority faction is what is to be avoided.

The principal danger posed by today's PC restricting free speech is that the voice of a majority faction can become too powerful if the other competing factions are being silenced. As Madison noted, the two main factions have always been those with and without the faculties to acquire property. The question remains, will the society fare better if it rewards those with or without faculties, abilities, and aptitudes? Is the role of government to protect property or redistribute property to buy votes? Despotism too often begins with the carrot of equality and ends with the stick of power's poison. As we will cover in Chapter 9, the equality of votes and treatment under the law are gifts from our Founding Fathers, but the equality of voters and opportunities is a delusion used ultimately to sell slavery. As long as it is easier to disable than create abilities, as long as it is easier to turn the able into idiots than to make idiots able, the truest equality will be found in death.

And while it is true that this is only one side of the story, if this side cannot be told, then there is only one side of the story left—a sure road to a majority faction and our loss of liberty.

FREEDOM OF BOYCOTT—FREEDOM OF SPEECH

In our chapter "Laughing at Political Correctness," one way we defined PC was as "replacing freedom of speech with freedom of boycott." Happily, this section will share how to embrace both freedoms at the same time.

Attend the tale of baseball great Curt Schilling,[22] a member of the 3000-strikeout club—one hot pitcher. In 2016, while a baseball analyst for ESPN, Schilling deplorably shared a Facebook post of a man in a wig and dress and the words, "LET HIM IN! to the restroom with your daughter or else you are a narrow-minded, judgmental, unloving racist bigot who needs to die."

I understand completely. As I get older, I pee more often. Recently I bought a pair of Keds shoes. As we know, "Keds are for Kids"—and women. I am no longer a kid, but no matter. This way, if I really have to pee and the men's room is occupied, I can—protected by PC and my magical transgender shoes—claim that I'm searching for the sex of my inner child in the women's room. Life, of course, is concerned with me—only me. I am entitled by my handicap, so others' discomfort is immaterial—my peeing problem is theirs; their embarrassment, not mine. Just to play it safe, however, I prefer gas-station single occupancy women's rooms—I hate being laughed at when I'm not trying to be funny.

Back to Schilling: he is obviously deplorable and proud and possibly has no empathy for the bladder deprived. He added to the Facebook post, "A man is a man no matter what they call themselves. I don't care what they are, who they sleep with, men's room was designed for the penis, women's not so much. Now you need laws telling us differently? Pathetic."[23]

Schilling had a valid anatomical point, not that the point protected him from the wrath of PC. Rather than ESPN simply providing a disclaimer that they neither agreed with nor were responsible for the opinions of their staff (any more than author David Cook is responsible for the opinions in his deplorable book), ESPN instead kowtowed to PC with the statement, "Curt Schilling has been advised that his conduct was unacceptable and his employment with ESPN has been terminated."

Such is the power of the new terrorism. PC threatens to turn freedom of speech into freedom of boycott. It is time to end the terrorism. Boycott need not be a one-way street. If every viewer of ESPN who believes in freedom of speech had written a note or cancelled his subscription, the new terrorism might have stopped then and there. Corporations might have begun to think twice before suppressing the noncorporate speech of their employees. The gag order of groupthink may have been lifted.

The First Amendment comes first; our freedom of speech must never be put second. Of all our rights—imagined and real—freedom of speech is senior, because freedom of speech is essential for protecting our other liberties. Representation in our government, equal protection of property under the law, our right to choose or reject eternity as we wish (at least until we get there)—all depend for their protection on the equality of our freedom of speech.

When American citizens were denied the vote by poll taxes and various other contrivances and shenanigans, it was freedom of speech that restored their voting privileges. When the life and property of American citizens dangled beneath oak trees and unequal protection by the law, it was freedom of speech that made the inequalities known. When Joseph McCarthy suppressed Americans' political beliefs under the excuse of warding off the threat of a Communist revolution, it was free speech that ended McCarthy's reign of terror—so that half a century later PC's suppression of free speech could allow the revolution to continue without complaint.

As David Cole, Georgetown law professor and National Legal Director of the ACLU, reminds us, "Where would the movements for racial justice, women's rights, and LGBT equality be without a muscular First Amendment." And, as

Cole advises, "the most powerful response to speech that we hate is not suppression but more speech."[24]

When forbidden by parents to listen, any child instinctively knows that it is time to perk up ears, take mental notes, and get ready for the blushing, for so long as free speech prevails there is nothing covered that shall not be revealed; and hid, that shall not be known. Sure, our abilities to speak are not equal; our stated ideas are not equal; but our freedom of speech—dumb, stammering, adroit, or eloquent; passionate, heartfelt, hypocritical, or deceitful; wise, reflective, impulsive, or foolish—is not only equal but must remain so to ward off the advance of tyranny.

To champion free speech demands exalting the freedom, not sanctioning the sentiments. Free speech is a bargain; worthless speech, an extravagance. Each citizen must be free to distinguish the bargains from the extravagances. Freedom deserves our respect; speech, our skepticism or belief, our praise, disinterest, or scorn. Censorship alone truly deserves our censure; censors, our intolerance, disdain, and disapproval, for threatening free speech threatens to rip asunder the very fabric of not only our lives, but our republic. In other words, those with nothing to say but what we shouldn't say, those who argue against free speech, should join the bakery shop owners and just shut up!

CHAPTER 8

TOLERANCE—
MAKING THE SALE, NOT BUYING THE BELIEF

> Understanding does not mean acceptance, and it
> does not necessarily mean respect. I don't say that all
> religious views are worthy of respect. I do claim that
> we should tolerate them, so long as they fall within the
> rule of law. Toleration implies that one objects to what
> is being tolerated, not that one respects or admires it.
>
> —*Tim Crane*

Love of money may be the root of all evil, but the root of all tolerance is the Latin *tolerare*, meaning "to bear or endure." To tolerate is to bear or endure pain, hardship, drugs, climate change, or other folk's religions—usually for love or money. Nothing demands tolerance quite like making love or money. For the right kiss or enough money, we will bear or endure just about any hardship. The face of Helen of Troy launched a thousand ships. Think of all that seasickness. Think of the Trojan horse and all those splinters.

Tolerance is also the principal lubricant of commerce. In the ancient world, merchants traveled what we now call the "silk road." The road's trade routes stretched from Japan to the Mediterranean Sea. The merchants of such far-flung lands were obviously not united in their cultural heritages. They were united in their quest for money, united in their desire to make the sale. To make that sale and money, they had to tolerate an enormous diversity of opinion, custom, and perversion.

I am blessed with a sixty-year history practicing tolerance for the sake of making sales. When I was five years old, I lived outside of Chicago in a little town not far from the Joliet Federal Prison. My hometown of one thousand offered the best of both worlds: two churches and two bars.

This was back in the days before the media had trained us all on the art of school shootings, poisoning unsealed containers, and practicing every other form of violence known to man. Without fear, I used to go door to door selling strawberries. I learned to tolerate pulling my wagon and enduring the comments about my cuteness long enough to walk away with twenty-five cents for each carton sold. I even tolerated splitting the income with my older brother who did the back-breaking work of stooping to pick the berries from the family patch.

By the time I was twelve years old, the family had moved to sunny Long Beach, California. I used to skin-dive off Rainbow Pier. Neither my youth nor Rainbow Pier still exists this side of memory, but at the time I would remove starfish from the pilings and prepare them for sale. The uncured starfish would stink, worse the longer they were out of the water. Transforming them into tolerable home decorations included boiling, scraping, and sunning them for weeks until the last of the strong odors had dissipated. The process took a degree of tolerance. In time, I found it was easier to sell the starfish to tourists on the beach, including instructions on how the creatures were to be cured.

I remember one customer in particular. She had pretty legs. She asked if she could store the starfish in her trunk on the train until reaching her home in the Midwest. Tolerating her stupidity (not to mention my own culpability), I said, "Of course." If she is alive today she must be well into her eighties. I wonder if she remembers tolerating the faults of a little boy. In any case, my conscience got the better of me and molded me into a more honest salesman.[1]

Whether we are making love or money, tolerance rules; pragmatism trumps ideology; we learn to lose every argument but win the sale. Suppose, for instance, we hope to make a living selling cheese. A customer walks up and begins to cite the latest conspiracy theory for why the moon is made of green cheese. Knowing the customer is always right, we listen attentively, nod at appropriate places in the story, and indicate that we understand exactly what the customer is saying. If he wants to mistake our nodding and tolerance for agreement, that's okay too. In sales, it's wise to suffer fools gladly.

When the customer finishes his tale, we say, entirely truthfully, "Yes, I've heard my whole life that the moon is made of green cheese. My father told me when I was about six years old." The customer smiles, happy to have found a comrade in arms against the green-cheese government cover-up. We then continue, "Our cheese is from Wisconsin, not the moon, and it's yellow, not green, but everyone loves it. How 'bout trying a sample?" We tolerate the green cheese, make the sale, and love the gold.

It makes no difference what comes out of the customer's mouth. If he tells us that Brazil is in Europe, or that Martians are the stupidest people in the universe, or that he's thinking about marrying his mother, we still nod, indicate our understanding of his remarks, and offer the cheese sample.

Sometimes people think they have to be right. They lack the wisdom to suffer fools. If someone tells them something that they imagine to be false, they just have to protest. They fill their lives and everyone else's with an intolerable quest for defending the truth of facts that make no difference to the circumstances at hand. These people have no ability to tolerate, bear, or endure errors. Their singleness of vision can make them dependable assets in our lives, but they have no business in sales. In sales, the game is won by making the sale, not by proving we are correct about the facts of the world. The only facts the salesman is responsible for are the facts about his product (unless the fool is a scientist and imagines his product is the facts of the world).

If the customer says that he's heard that cheese does not have to be kept in the refrigerator, we would find it incumbent to insist, "I can't say what is true about other cheeses, but this one you have to keep cool, or it will spoil. But it's delicious, isn't it? Storing it in the refrigerator won't be that big of a deal. The cheese's special taste is worth the inconvenience. How would you like to pay for that, cash or card?"

Love and money may demand tolerance, but, if carried to the extreme, the love of tolerance is no less evil than the love of money. Ignoring errors of fact is one thing; believing errors of truth; quite another.

Facts are fleeting. One day, Pluto is a planet; the next, an oversize chunk of ice to be shaken not stirred in a cosmic

James Bond's vodka martini. One day, anvils fall because of gravity; the next, they fall because of warps in space time. One day, the heavens are immutable; the next day they are expanding. One day, continents are fixed; the next day, they are floating. One day, time is absolute; the next day, it is relative. One day, light is a wave; the next, a particle; the next, both. One day, Copernicus assures us that our sun is the center of the universe; the next day, we are not even certain that the universe has a center. Facts come and go. They are a contrivance of pragmatism, no better than the miracles of physical science they allow.

Truth is of a different ilk. Truth does not change. In Saint Anselm's "Ontological Argument," God is "a being than which nothing greater can be conceived." According to such a definition, the limits of our conceptions may change but God will not. As Anselm wrote:

> I do not endeavor, O Lord, to penetrate your sublimity, for in no wise do I compare my understanding with that; but I long to understand in some degree your truth, which my heart believes and loves. For I do not seek to understand that I may believe, but I believe in order to understand.[2]

If you are a saint, I imagine you can readily agree; if not, philosophies on truth vary. We'll consider only two at this time, saving some others for later.

In ancient Greece, there were two main schools of philosophical thought. One school was dominated by Socrates and Plato who taught that truth was absolute—though darn hard to find more than approximated here on earth. The other school was controlled by itinerant teachers known as sophists who taught that philosophy was all about sales and that the truth that would make the sale in Athens might be different than the truth that would make the sale in Sparta. For the sophists, truth was relative. Because Socrates and Plato were the better salesmen, the notion of yet-to-be-fully-grasped absolute truth won out, for a time at least, in philosophy.[3]

Today, both the absolute and relative views of truth continue to thrive. For Christians, steeped in absolutism, it is always correct to love our brothers and sisters—but it's not okay to date them. Dating them requires relative truth. In the relative story, it may be fine to date our sisters. According to the story, our current age is the most enlightened, and enlightenment dictates we make our own moral choices. Every child, the relativists claim, should be encouraged to decide for himself if anatomy and nature got it wrong. He has the right to explore and decide if he prefers the men's or women's locker room; the right to explore if he is right or left handed; the right to determine if he prefers sodomy, incest, bestiality, polygamy; and the right to explore whether he prefers the taste of human flesh and wants to attend the Jeffrey Dahmer Culinary Institute. How will he—the relative story goes—know what he really likes if he is discouraged from exploration?

If, however, we believe that truth is absolute and there are absolute limits when it comes to kissing our sisters, then when it comes to making the Wisconsin cheese sale, we may have to tolerate progressive consensus on moon-cheese conspiracies, but only for the sake of love or money. We have no duty to condone, respect, or believe such conspiracies for any other reason outside of the sales cycle; we have no duty to bring the green-cheese theorist home to pervert the beliefs of our family; and we have no duty to teach our children to condone, respect, or believe green-cheese thought—even if such thought is billed (this year) as progressive. The itching from mosquito bites may demand our tolerance, but not our respect.

Remember, tolerance means making the sale, not buying the belief. We should never confuse tolerance with belief or allow toleration to confuse our beliefs. It is one thing to tolerate the itching of a phantom limb after a shark attack. It is quite another to convert to Zen Buddhism, abandon logical reasoning, and contemplate "the sound of one hand clapping." We need not confuse toleration with a conversion to Zen Buddhism nor salvation with enlightenment. Our families need not join the shark's tummy in applauding the sound of one hand digesting.

CHAPTER 9

THE EQUALITY DELUSION

No advance in wealth, no softening of manners, no
reform or revolution has ever brought human equality
a millimeter nearer.

—*George Orwell*

work with children who suffer from visual perception problems, difficulty discerning how things are alike and different. Many of these kids struggle with math. When I point to the equal sign and ask for its meaning, I'm assured it means "equal." When I ask what "equal" means, they frequently have no idea. To the perceptually challenged, equal signs are only marks on the page that tell us "where the answer goes." Needless to say, for such children math is a muddle. And then these children grow up to know everything about equality except what it means. In their calculations only one half of the equation need be equal. We call them egalitarians.[1] They suffer from a strange delusion that we will explore below.

DELUSION AND ILLUSION

What is a delusion? Both illusions and delusions are falsehoods. If we were to accompany the Oxy Morons in their stroll through the history of words, we would find that sometimes the words *illusion* and *delusion* are interchangeable, sometimes not. For our purposes, I'm going to divide them by sense, illusions belonging to eyes; delusions, to ears; perhaps more accurately, illusions belonging to images; delusions, to words.

Illusions result from borrowing our actions of seeing in habitual settings to performing the actions of seeing in novel settings. Suppose, for instance, that a child raised inside a windowless house were to take his first walk outside. Viewing a mountain, the child would likely do vision the same way he learned to do vision to navigate furniture, hallways, and staircases—the apparent sizes of the objects predicting the movement needed to reach them. As a result, he would have the illusion that the mountain was very close and that it could quickly be reached by walking, even though in fact the mountain was miles away. The mountain's nearby appearance is false, an illusion—much like the illusion that inspires us to chase rainbows.

Delusions are similarly caused by doing language in new settings as we did language in old settings. Suppose, for instance, we open a pillbox containing three pills, all visible, none hidden. Asked to "count *all* the pills in the box," we would understand the word *all* and correctly answer "three." Asked to "count *all* the stars in the sky" however, we would likely apply the word *all* to the stars the same way we applied *all* to the pills even though the *all* of the stars we can neither count nor imagine. The *all* of the pills directs action; the *all* of the stars deludes us into thinking we can conceive the limits of the universe.

The *all* of the pills provides but a metaphor or analogy for the *all* of the stars. The delusion is no different than saying,

"The woman is a hurricane" and expecting her to flood New Orleans. The same type of delusion plagues us when we swap the word *all*. Consider the question, "Can an *all*-powerful God create a stone He cannot lift?" Logically speaking, a Being either unable to create the stone or unable to lift it would not be *all*-powerful. In truth, it is not God's power that creates the problem; the problem is our delusion that words can necessarily transcend their actions, that counting *all* the pills is no different than understanding *all* of God's power, a power that could well exceed *all* mortal language and imagination—whatever that *all* means.

Such delusions are harmless, only becoming potentially dangerous when we are trying to sell something. To tell the parable of "*all* the pills in the box" in order to sell beachfront property on "*all* the stars in the sky" is, at best, equivocation; at worst, larceny. Rhetoricians, whether philosophers, politicians, or polemicists, wittingly or unwittingly confuse the definition of the star-*all* with the definition of box-*all*, especially if the delusion makes the sale.

Selling "*equality* for *all*" is much like selling "*all* the stars in the sky." Such *equality* is a delusion created in much the same way that the star-*all* delusion was created—by confusing the *equality* of numbers with the *equality* of qualities or by confusing "treating people *equally*" with "making people *equal*." The *equals* are hardly equal. To confuse them creates delusion.

Imagine, for instance, we have two pill boxes, each holding three easily counted pills. The quantity of the pills in each box is *equal*. This allows us to imagine that the quality of the pills is *equal*. Nothing could be further from the truth. The pills in one box could be Ritalin; in the other box, ex-lax. One box might overwhelm poopy behavior; the other box, create it. It is a delusion to imagine that *equal* quantities, be it pills, or pieces of the pie, are somehow equivalent to equal qualities—ability, goodness, tastiness, industry, etc. That we can count the pills in the box does not mean we can count the stars in the sky. And that we can count the pills in the two boxes as equal in number does not mean we can count them as equal in quality.

Similarly, we can pass laws so that the pills are treated equally, each pill requiring a prescription to be dispensed, but we cannot pass laws that makes all pills equal. Although bad laws can turn practically anything into poop, good laws cannot turn poop makers into poop reducers. Good laws treat people equally; they do not make people equal.

The nearest government can come to granting equality is to treat people equally, not abridge liberty by state coercion in the hopes of creating equal people. Laws designed to make unequal people equal create poop, not equality, not cultural revolution. Nothing revolves; the circle is merely truncated by swiping culture off the top like swiping whipped cream and marshmallows off the top of hot chocolate—to toss the best part down the drain.

The only way to treat people equally is to allow them to be unequal. The only way to make people equal is to treat them unequally—ignoring, reducing, or retarding one; enhancing or advancing another—even though those requiring us to lower the bar are often incapable of enhancement or advancement. Government can treat individuals equally, allowing each equal protection of property under the law; equal access to public facilities; equal freedom to speak, vote, or pray; and equal liberty from government intrusion and coercion. Governments cannot grant individuals equal faculties for acquiring equal property; governments cannot grant equal speaking skills, equal thinking skills, equal voting or praying wisdom.

Thus, government cannot create equal opportunities; fleeting opportunities are not equal to lasting opportunities, and lasting opportunities come as much from within as without, as much from our talents and industry as any environmental equality supplied by the government. Any opportunities granted would be fleeting for some, lasting for others, and, therefore, unequal. Given one bag of gold apiece, some would soon have ten; some, none. In this world, at least, opportunities are seldom equal.

To confuse *treating people equally* with *making people equal* or to confuse the *equality of numbers* with the *equality of qualities* are both examples of the equality delusion in action. Quite simply, the equality delusion is the game with no losers—except the winners. In this chapter, we will study the equality delusion (ED) and argue that the politically correct can no more turn delusion into truth than we can count the stars in the universe. To accomplish for this delusion what Marx has attempted for religion, allow me to borrow and revise the philosopher's words for our purposes: "The . . . [equality delusion] is the sigh of the oppressed creature, the heart of a heartless world, and the soul of soulless conditions. It is the opium of the people."[2] And without a doubt the ED is the opiate of the politically correct.

FAMILY VALUES

Before we fully expose the delusion, however, let me address some obvious objections to my favoring a government that treats us equally rather than attempts to make us equal. It can, for instance, be argued that delusions can inspire us. The argument has merit: pursuing the delusion of a three-minute mile could lead to untold records. But using the delusion to justify taking away our spirituality, free will, and free speech, or to deplore, denigrate, and dehumanize us as *speedists*—imagining and promoting our prejudice against speed—is more likely to weaken and enslave us than to generate three-minute miles.

Similarly, as parents eventually learn, it may or may not be possible to love and treat their children equally, but, short of filicide,[3] parents cannot make their children equal. Children were created with different gifts. When it comes to creating opportunities, the gifts may not be equal. That said, frequently parents do not treat their children equally. Just as the shepherd may spend more time searching for the one lost sheep than the ninety-nine grazing in the pasture, and just as a woman may devote more attention to one lost piece of silver than nine pieces lying safely on the table, so will a mother often devote her time to the child with the most difficulties even if that devotion means ignoring the enhancement of the rest.

This is the difference between a parent and a competitor. A winning coach will devote more time to the best players than to those on the bench. The coach treats the players equally, devoting equal time for equal talent and production, not equal moral worth. The coach with ten quarterbacks doesn't waste time trying to make them equal. As a result, all players win championships; all travel to the playoffs and finals; all receive bonuses, however unequal.

Is the job of government to protect life and property and make a nation competitive or to treat the citizens of the world as family—from each according to his ability, to each according to his need? Would we rather our nation, as its Founding Fathers intended, protected property and left us equally alone to get on with our work, moral commitments, and virtues; or would we rather the nation made us equal by reducing our resources to the highest bar that the lowest can vault? Should the government protect rather than control property, allowing the economic stream of competitive nature the liberty to flow as we swim, drown, or enrich our families or neighbors by inspiring their virtues and heart-given charity? Or should government coerce us under threat of imprisonment or violence, control rather than protect our property, and treat us all like family as we paddle against the flow of competitive nature, eventually faltering, sweeping back downstream, and beginning afresh like Sisyphus and his boulder?

As a nation, we are divided on how to answer these questions, and, who knows, maybe this is best. As we paddle against each other, going nowhere allows the triumph of conservatism. Still, families give us children, and competition turns life into a game. Before deciding between a competitive or paternalistic government, consider the nature of family.

How often, benevolent or not, is a family despotic? How often are parents the dictators so long as they control the purse strings and muscle?[4] How often, without a warrant, do they search under the mattress for contraband; censor books or the Internet to control our minds; set curfews and subject us to corporal punishment or time-out? How often do they choose our friends and religion? Do we really want a government that treats us like family, especially a family that will allow us neither to grow up nor move out on our own? Families prepare us for the world and set us free. Governments prepare us for unending taxes. Do we want to be treated equally, or do we want to be made equal? With those questions as preface, we will continue our study of the ED.

EQUAL QUANTITY VERSUS EQUAL QUALITY

The word *equal* comes from the Latin *aequus* meaning "level, even, equal." If your table top is *even*, your marbles will continue to roll when pushed. When it comes to such evenness, levelness, or equality of quantity, we are generally talking about numbers. Suppose a man and woman share equal chest and waist sizes: forty-inch chests, twenty-eight-inch waists. We would say their chest and waist sizes are equal. To extend sameness from quantities to qualities, however, demands a leap of faith.

In the physical world, quantities can be equal, qualities cannot. No two objects are really alike, even, level, or equal. The quarks just won't hold still. And since science assures us that not just women but all of us are objects, then none of us are equal—physically speaking. And since science also assures us that minds are just brains, then no two minds can be equal either because no two brains have an equal distribution of cells. Thus, we can be equal in neither body nor mind—at least if we are being scientific enough to believe that the metaphors of science can be incorporated as a wonderful tool for conquering the physical world and a wonderful rhetorical tool for creating delusions about what it means to be human.[5]

In the above example of our man and woman, equality of measurements says nothing about equality of qualities. The man, for instance, could be a slender transvestite with an oversize breast implant. The woman could be a championship, steroid-laden body builder, benching two times her weight. Equality in the mathematical sense says nothing about equality in the qualitative sense. Quite simply, equal numbers do not equate with equal qualities. This is why the ED favors mathematical equality, and stacks the deck with progressive taxation or racial quotas to achieve it, penalizing the able in favor of the "equal." In truth, as PC understands, the only way we can make people equal is to turn them into numbers, whether as votes, quotas, incomes, or percentages of a community. To reduce people to numbers is an example of the ED hard at work.

What, for instance, would it tell us about equality if in the United States Senate there were fifty male senators and fifty female senators? Their quantity would be equal. But would the senators really be equal? What percentage of the women who began the process were elected? If a woman had to be twice as good as a man to win an election, then the numbers would tell us nothing about equality of quality. If, however, the nation has a strong penchant for affirmative action, so that to win an election a woman only had to be half as good as a man, then, again, the numbers would tell us nothing about equality. And the use of numbers to promote the ED would not tell us if things were getting better or worse (especially since, when resources are limited, better for one typically means worse for another).

The concept of equality of quality becomes more and more confusing the more we explore. Such equality refers to rank, power, and excellence. And excellence, in turn, is even more confusing, referring as it does to uncommon goodness, surpassing ability, superior merit, exceptional worth, or outstanding skill in relationships. Quite a hodgepodge of possible equalities to compare. Quite a hodgepodge to capture with numbers selected to sell the ED.

EQUAL WORTH VERSUS EQUAL VALUE

According to the popularizer of capitalism, Adam Smith, water has worth, since we cannot live without it; diamonds have value. In a town whose streets are paved with diamonds the size of cobblestones, the value of one-carat diamonds might be deflated when compared to one-carat diamonds in our own stone cobblestone society.

We should not confuse worth and value. Christ might allow that the drunk sleeping outside my office door has the same moral worth that I do sleeping behind my desk. That the drunk and I have equal moral worth in no way implies we have equal value to my office staff. As the staff might confess, the drunk has superior value: he is a sounder sleeper and thus gets in the way less.

That we are equal in moral worth in the eyes of a loving God does not make us equal in value to society any more than God's equal love for you and me guarantees any of us central air-conditioning for eternity. Worth is not value. That we receive equal treatment under the rule of law requires that Beyoncé Knowles and I receive equal fines for equal violations of the speed limit. Unequal treatment by the law to equalize our singing abilities would be an example of the ED. The state would be deluded to flush money down the toilet to fund my vocal lessons. And no matter how much it hurts my feelings that others prefer Beyoncé's singing to mine, it would be tyranny to tax audiences to pay equal compensations for our performances, despite my psychological needs. In truth, only the removal of our vocal cords could make Beyoncé and me equal as vocalists, and equal dance skills would require no less than cremation. Equality demands reduction of all to the lowest common denominator. In Aldous Huxley's words, "That all men are equal is a proposition to which, at ordinary times, no sane human being has ever given his assent."[6] To believe otherwise is delusion.

EQUAL OPPORTUNITY

In a better world, equality in one quality would be correlated with equality in another. But this is not that better world. If it were, those with excellence in goodness, ability, or merit would surely excel in rank and recompense. Such equality touches on the concepts of justice and fairness, but the world is neither just nor fair. Anyone with an inkling about life can tell us that the only competition that is fair is the one in which we compete against ourselves. Our opportunities, providence, or fate (take your pick) are just not fair. Some are born healthy, smart, and happy; some, sick, dumb, and sad. Some are dealt deuces; some, a royal flush. Only our opportunities for arrogance are equal, because no one but God is playing with a full deck.[7]

What the ED hides is that the *happiness* in the *pursuit of happiness* is in the pursuit, not the wealth of opportunities. The pursuit of anguish is in the excuses, not the dearth of opportunities. The opportunities that make us happiest are the ones we created, not the ones we were given. The immigrant taking responsibility to attain citizenship is far happier than the natural citizen taking citizenship for granted. The joy in an opportunity rests not in the opportunity but in taking responsibility for the opportunity. Unless, perhaps, we succumb to the sin of envy, building the smallest fortune brings happiness; squandering the largest inheritance brings only sorrow.

Our failures rest not in a lack of luck or opportunities but in not taking responsibility to add to the world everything our opportunities allow. A bagboy with Down syndrome excelling at his job has a better chance for happiness than a Harvard graduate drinking and womanizing rather than taking the reins of his business. We are responsible for what we do with our opportunities today. There is no one but ourselves to blame if we waste an opportunity—however unequal those opportunities are compared to those of others. Time spent envying the opportunities of others is time wasted on excuses rather than excelling to the limits of our own opportunities.

The ED assures us, falsely, that happiness depends on equal opportunity rather than uncommon responsibility; if we all could win the lottery or the government could redistribute the wealth of billionaires, we'd all be equally happy. Such thinking is the ED, utter nonsense, as ridiculous as yearning for retirement. There is far more joy to be found in achievement than retirement. The joy of wealth is in creating it or using it to add to the world; the joy is not to be found in death or taxes, no matter how inevitable they may be.

The disparity between equality of merit and equality of success is hardly new news. Life has never been fair. In Ecclesiastes 9:11 we find, "I returned, and saw under the sun, that the race is not to the swift, nor the battle to the strong, neither yet bread to the wise, nor yet riches to men of understanding, nor yet favour to men of skill; but time and chance happeneth to them all." Thus, although our excellence is not equal, there is still hope for true equality for "*there is one event unto all . . . they go* to the dead." When it comes to death, we share and share alike. Equality for all, not, as already mentioned, that the afterlife promises all an apartment with a view—and central air-conditioning.

This linking of equality outside of life has a long history. We are created equal before we get here and will return to equality when we leave. Publius's first Maxim stated in the century before Christ, "As men we are all equal in the presence of death."[8] John Donne wrote, "Death comes equally to us all, and makes us all equal when it comes."[9] The entertainer Bob Dylan concurred centuries later, "All this talk of equality. The only thing people really have in common is that they are all going to die."[10] And Mark Twain, reaching his mortal end, shared best in his last written words, "Death, the only immortal who treats us all alike, whose pity and whose peace and whose refuge are for all—the soiled and the pure, the rich and the poor, the loved and the unloved."

In a better world, we are all equal. And dead. At least that's one viewpoint. There is also the viewpoint, known variously as "karma,";"What goes around comes around," and "We reap what we sow." Or as cult leader Claire Winfield Kelly expressed it in my novel *The Anatomy of Blindness*, "What we create for others, we create for ourselves." If we talk to Lucifer, we may hear complaints that some are still less equal than others even after shedding their skins.

MUCH ADO ABOUT NOTHING

The ED requires the equality of all. That, I imagine, should include the equality of all geometric forms. Were such the case, the following syllogism would ring true: *All circles are squares; all squares are round; therefore, all circles are round.* The logic is valid, the conclusion is true, and from the one-dimensional perspective of the ED even the premises are true because all geometric forms can be made equal by a government with the correct perspective.

If you have doubts on this equality, draw a circle and a square on a piece of paper. Turn the paper horizontal to the ground with the geometric figures closer to the ceiling. Raise the paper until it is at the exact height of your eyes and stare at the edge of the paper. Now, recall that, in Euclid's world at least, circles and squares have only two dimensions: height and width. They have no third dimension, no depth. In Euclid's geometry, the paper is infinitely thin. Thus, the ED works just fine in one-dimensional thinking in a one-dimensional world where all shapes are truly equal. When it comes to Euclidian circles and squares there is nothing in the third dimension. And nothing equals nothing. Both being nothing, the circle and square are equal, but only from the perspective of those living in the sophisticated, one-dimensional world of the ED.

In the same way that the circle and square, viewed from the side, are both equal to nothing and therefore equal to each other, the ED similarly requires that we view our wealthier neighbors as nothing. From the perspective of the delusion, we are all nothing. Only then can all be equal. You cannot turn a mindless imbecile into a genius, but you can turn a genius into a mindless imbecile; all it takes is the big enough cudgel of a big enough government. The ED always demands the lowest common denominator because that's the only denominator that the common and the lowliest can reach.[11]

Cultural revolutions bring "equality" not by elevating peasants but by eliminating the cultured. The delusion demands the imbecility of geniuses because such equality makes power much easier to come by for the true elite. And yes, there are always the elite—those like Hitler, Stalin, or Mao who somehow manage to fall outside of the delusion to become more equal than the rest. Confusing treating people equally with making people equal demands a perspective that turns everyone into nothing. And thus, the death and logic metaphors arrive at the same conclusion: The ED equals death.

NATURAL VERSUS LEGISLATED RIGHTS

As we noted when we began, to explore natural rights try swimming in a tsunami. Legislated rights cannot suspend natural rights no matter what those enamored of the ED insist. Natural rights demand that not even equality can allow two cars to occupy the same parking space at the same time. No legislative effort or traffic sign can allow such "double parking" or create any other right that does not exist in nature. Our legislated equality with birds cannot grant us the natural right to fly. Again, no law can turn morons into geniuses, just geniuses into morons.

The *Declaration of Independence*, written by a committee including the good racist Thomas Jefferson, allows, "We hold these truths to be self-evident, that all men are created equal."[12] Then what happened? Only God knows. Was Jefferson's rhetorical flourish meant to sell our revolution to Europe, or did he really believe that all men had equal rights when it came to dating their slaves? Was Jefferson speaking of our equality under the law, or did he imagine that he and his nemesis Alexander Hamilton were cut from the exact same cloth?

Jefferson was hardly the first to reflect on the equality of men. Two millennia earlier, Aristotle captured the nature of our equality when he wrote, "Democracy arises out of the notion that those who are equal in any respect are equal in all respects; because men are equally free, they claim to be absolutely equal." Aristotle, who did not care for direct democracy, apparently understood the ED. It is unlikely he subscribed to the notion that equality under the law suggests a natural equality of value, goodness, ability, merit, intelligence, talent, or skill in relationships. In other words, Aristotle was skeptical that the equality of votes could guarantee the equality of voters. Votes are counted by numbers, but other than to politicians, numbers are not what make people count.

The politically correct pursuit of the ED interprets Jefferson to mean that not only are we equal in the eyes of God and the law, but we must also be equal in the eyes of the employer. A different way to view Jefferson's words is that America is like a football game. Your citizenship purchases your ticket for a seat, but you are responsible for your own sack lunch. Your pursuit of happiness is your right to try to earn your way onto the playing field. This is based on your talent, not your ticket. All tickets are equal. All talents are not.

There is yet another way to interpret Jefferson's "created equal"—the metaphor of the ED horserace.

In the delusion, it is the government's job to see to it that all horses are created equal. Dark red, Thoroughbred race horse; fifty-five-mile-per-hour quarter horse; Appaloosa with its beautiful spotted coat that would have made Joseph jealous; 2,200 pound Clydesdale draft horse, standing seventy-two inches tall; Percheron war horse, weighing 2,600 pounds; white mustang, feral and free; miniature horse, less than thirty-four inches tall; Shetland pony, twenty-eight to forty-two inches high—all are equal.

But how are they equal? Must the horses be handicapped in a way that photo finishes are always necessary—especially because, getting bored, the spectators have all gone home? Should the Thoroughbreds be cropped at the knee and the miniature horses given stilts? And why not dye all the horses black so that white, bay, chestnut, Appaloosa leopard spotted, grey, brindle, buckskin, dun, and palomino gold will not distract from the equality? In time, all the horses can be interbred until their highfalutin claims to individuality and heritage can be lost into equality.

While the politically correct worship diversity, in the ED horse world, equine diversity must end; breeding, other than interbreeding, should be halted; it is hardly fair for a horse to have the unequal advantage of being sired by a Seabiscuit. On the racetrack of equality all advantages of heredity must be curtailed. And what about training? Why should the Thoroughbred receive the best training? Why not the miniatures, who need the extra advantage? All racetrack signs should be written, not only in Thoroughbred but in quarter horse, miniature horse, Clydesdale, and maybe Shetland pony. And how about the mustangs? What gives them the right to a freedom unequal to the rest? They all need to be captured, broken, and corralled just like everyone else. And every horse deserves a wreath of flowers at the end of each race so that no horse will have his feelings hurt. In a truly equal racetrack, the spectators will also be presented with wreaths of their own.

In the ED, the thrill of the race is not in running one's heart out; the thrill is in equality of opportunity and equality of outcome despite diversity of heart and talent. The perfect world envisioned by delusion would run on equality, not competition. And yet, as the eighty million deaths created by

Stalin and Mao demonstrate, equality is the competition to end all competitions, with the more equal controlling from on top the play of the less equal contentedly working their way to becoming truly equal—with dust. But then Stalin and Mao were experts at not only the delusion of equality, but at using PC to suspend spirituality, free will, and freedom of speech. Under the paternal dictators, all were equal—when they died. Who could ask for anything more: except, maybe, to remain deplorable and proud.

CHAPTER 10

RELATIONSHIPS—WHAT DO YOU SAY WHEN YOU CAN'T SAY NO?

A relationship, I think, is like a shark, you know? It
has to constantly move forward or it dies.
And I think what we got on our hands
is a dead shark.

—Woody Allen

In our Bill Cosby chapter, we noted that the comedian allegedly slipped chemistry into the crescendos of his romantic overtures. If such melodies actually happened, they would be considered rape. Why? Because rape removes the victim's possibly most cherished right: the right to say no to a relationship. Not even the beast in *Beauty and the Beast* or the prince in *The Princess and the Frog* could break their spells without performing that sales ritual known as "wooing the girl." Kissing the girl without making her cry takes work. Bypassing the work is rape. Such are the demands of legitimately establishing a relationship. Let me assure you, I never left out the wooing before I married anyone—I wooed them all.

So, what's so important about relationship? Aristotle claimed it was our reason that made us human. Nonsense. It was our parents who made us human. Knowledge, however, was also key. They knew each other, or we would not be here. The most important knowledge we can obtain is the knowledge of another person. This ranks above the knowledge of the heavens, except perhaps for one, and even that heaven revolves around our relationship with God through our relationship with our neighbors. If God is truth, then truth revolves around relationship. The easiest way to love our neighbors is to move to a smaller neighborhood, one to which, we can hope, the politically correct—or, if one is politically correct, the deplorable and proud—do not have the key.

Philosophy is the love of wisdom. The wisdom of the world is for naught if one is alone in the world. The greatest philosophy ever written is worthless and valueless to a sole survivor dying of loneliness. Yet, of course, it could be argued that person, pen, and page have a relationship of sorts. We learn about ourselves and others as we write, but what we learn would have no value without the hope of relationship. Aristotle claimed we are political animals. Indeed, with the exception of a few of the longer wavelengths on the autism spectrum, we are relationship-oriented beasts. Even a misanthrope's world would seem empty with no one left to hate.

RELATIONSHIPS MAKE THE WORLD GO ROUND

It turns out that nothing is more sacred than relationship. Relationship is more important than ownership. A man could own the entire world, but if he had no one with whom to share it, he would have nothing. God concurred.[1] It's even been said that who you know is more important that what you know. This is also true. An author can write the most lyrical, wise, and profound book, but without the relationship with a reader, the writing is for naught other than the author's amusement. He might as well waste his time playing videogames on Mars.

Homes, cities, nations, and worlds revolve around relationship. Without relationship, a house is not a home; a planet is not a world. Gravity makes a planet go round, but relationship makes the world go round. Without relationship, a city becomes a ruin; a nation becomes a wasteland.

We learn to read and write for the purpose of relationship. We learn to speak for the purpose of relationship. Language and communication, words and stories revolve around relationship. Even petting the family pooch revolves around relationship.

Everything we are taught in school revolves around relationship. Engineering allows the building of buildings. Buildings are built for the purpose of shelter, but also for the purpose of encouraging the relationships we want and restricting the relationships we don't. The knowledge we learn in school may, at times, appear useless, but every subject, no matter how arcane, includes words, and words build relationships. Even if a subject is blatantly false, learning it will expand our relationship with a teacher, school, and profession.

Morality hinges on relationship. The Christian story begins with a broken relationship and ends with a restored relationship. The Abrahamic religions began with the choice of one relationship over another.

PROPERTY RIGHTS AND RELATIONSHIP

Having touched on the primacy of relationship in our lives, let's return to our good racist, sexist friend Thomas Jefferson. He said that God created us with the inalienable rights of life, liberty, and the pursuit of happiness. We don't really know exactly what Jefferson meant by happiness, but he was a fan of English philosopher John Locke. Locke speculated that we have a basic right to our property, providing we don't use various forms of force or deceit to harm the person or property of another. For Locke, we have a natural right to life, liberty, and property.

Whether or not Jefferson's *happiness* was a euphemism for Locke's *property*, we don't really know. But we can explore some of Locke's words about property and see that, for Locke, property was more than real estate, more than location, location, location. Property, in a sense, was about relationship, relationship, relationship:

> Though the Earth, and all inferior Creatures be common to all Men yet every Man has a *Property* in his own *Person*. This no Body has any Right to but himself. The *Labour* of his Body, and the *Work* of his Hands, we may say, are properly his. Whatsoever then he removes out of the State that Nature hath provided, and left it in, he hath mixed with his own *Labour* with, and joyned to it something that is his own, and thereby makes it his *Property*.[2]

In Locke's view, God gave the earth and the trees and animals to us all in common. But if I venture out into nature and with my own hands pick a basket of deplorables[3] or other nuts, then those nuts are my property and you would do well to keep your hands off my nuts unless you are fixin' to feel the blunt edge of my other property, that stone I recently fashioned into a bludgeon.

What's important is that Locke suggested we have a relationship with our property, just as I have a relationship with my socks and my underwear and the optometric practice I have built and my favorite tie that I have decorated with Vietnamese food at the bidding of my contrary chopsticks. Thus the *property* Locke[4] is referring to is more like our possessions, our well-worn slippers or favorite sweater, or the car washed weekly by our own hands.

You may not have knit the sweater, but you have nonetheless established a relationship with it, just as you have established a relationship with your car and home. Following Locke's lead, Jefferson should have described our inalienable rights to include the pursuit of—not *happiness*, not *property*, but—*relationship*. There is nothing more sacred than relationship.

And this is why our most important, God given, inalienable right is the right to accept or reject a relationship. God granted us free will so we may accept or reject a relationship even with Him. God's love is a gift, but we never feel His kiss without our consent. *That* would be rape.

GOVERNMENT FORCE AND FREE RELATIONSHIPS

If you look at the times that religion has gone awry, it is when God's gift of love has been forced upon us by our hateful neighbors. It is when we have been raped in the name of God by people who don't know Him. The Inquisitions and Crusades were examples of love being replaced with rape enforced by government. American slavery was rape enforced by government. Slaves were given no choice about accepting or rejecting the relationship imposed upon them. The federal government and its Fugitive Slave Act of 1850 turned enforced relationship between slave and slave owner into a federal rather than only local tyranny. The bloodiest war in American history could be viewed either as an attempt to restrict states from rejecting a relationship with the federal government or an attempt to allow blacks to reject relationships with slave owners. Was Lincoln more interested in perpetuating the rape of the states or eliminating the rape of the slaves to justify perpetrating the bloodiest war in American history?

Either way, local governments and the private terror and violence of groupthink established segregation to take away free will in the choice of relationships; kisses between white and black lips were made illegal by the anti-miscegenation laws of government, not to mention the groupthink that, back then, passed as PC. The choice or rejection of relationship was again no longer a choice—it was law. And government and its laws just kept on taking choice after choice of relationship out of our hands.

In the 1930s Roosevelt's New Deal enforced segregation. After World War II, when an increasingly liberal government, instead of protecting property decided to build it, the public housing built was, by federal law, segregated. In what became the suburbs, the federal government insured loans for mortgages, but only in segregated neighborhoods—again taking freedom of choice out of accepting or rejecting a relationship. As Richard Rothstein, a fellow at the Thurgood Marshall Institute of the National Association for the Advancement of Colored People's legal defense fund argues, it was not freely chosen private prejudice, white flight, income differences, or self-segregation that most fostered segregation. It was government:

> [*De facto* segregation (individually decided acceptance or rejection of relationship)] remains a small part of the truth, submerged by a far more important one: until the last quarter of the twentieth century, racially explicit policies of federal, state and local governments defined where whites and African Americans should live. Today's residential segregation in the North, South, Midwest, and West is not the unintended consequences of individual choices . . . but of unhidden public policy that explicitly segregated every metropolitan area in the United States.[5]

What goes around comes around. What we reap we sow. Karma always arrives in the mail even though Buddhists assure us there is no self with his name on the mailbox. The refusal of our government's law enforcement to protect equally the life and property of the colorless and colorful allowed terror, violence, or the threat of violence by groupthink. Government officials repressed our natural right to accept or reject relationships. Today, government uses affirmative action for the same purpose—forced rather than wooed relationships. Such forced relationships were and are bitterly contested. They cannot be protested, however, because just as yesterday's politically correct groupthink denied freedom of speech against segregation, today's politically correct groupthink denies freedom of speech against integration. Our freedom freely to accept or reject relationships is still not our own.

PC continues to sell the idea that if government can screw things up, then more and bigger government can set them right. To laud integration gets things backwards. Like wealth, integration is an outcome, not a cause, not a reason for an outcome. Wealth that is earned brings happiness. Wealth that is unearned does not. Similarly, integration that results from individuals making free choices brings happiness. Taking away the basic right to accept or reject relationships does not.

While PC wastes time on dreams of integration, most of us, whatever the color of our skin, merely want to live in a safe neighborhood with comfortable homes convenient to jobs, amenities, and excellent schools. We want to be treated equally under the law, our lives and property protected with equal vigor. When we are not, we have every reason to protest.

In actuality, integration is more often like the play of toddlers; although all sit on the floor of the same room, each plays a game of his own imagination. If we want to see how important integration itself is to most of us—black, white, purple, or green—take a poll to determine what percentage of us invite members of other races to share dinner at our homes.

Like charity, love is a gift—including a gift to ourselves. When we love, we discover our souls. Being loved enriches us with the overflow from one who has discovered the best of himself. Neither charity nor love can be legislated. A required show of affection is worthless to anyone. Genuine self-generated affection blesses both the loved and the lover. With grace from on high, love may triumph, and the gift be returned. It can never be compelled, forced, enforced, obliged, imposed, or coerced by strength of public opinion, fear of boycott, or the threats of PC or governments. Love and any other relationship must be freely given and accepted. Love is an opportunity for transcendence, not a duty. To not love is to lose the better part of our souls, but to legislate relationships is but one step away from legislating rape. Such legislation and legislators will not endure.

CHAPTER 11

XENOPHOBIA, NATIVISM, AND COMMON SENSE

"Give me your tired, your poor,
Your huddled masses yearning to breathe free,
The wretched refuse of your teeming shore.
Send these, the homeless, tempest-tost to me,
I lift my lamp beside the golden door!"

—*Emma Lazarus*

While it is unwise to scorn a 305-foot woman carrying a torch for anyone or any cause, it is amusing to find how the words *wretched refuse* are somehow overlooked to promote the more poetic "huddled masses yearning to breathe free" whenever Lazarus's Statue-of-Liberty poem is quoted. Such is the power of fallacious rhetoric to appeal to emotion. In this chapter, we will lament those wretched xenophobes and nativists and all who seek to exclude the wretched refuse from teeming on our shores.

XENOPHOBIA

"Don't be a stranger!"

Good advice. Show me someone who claims not to be afraid of strangers and I'll show you a moron or a liar. If none of us were afraid of strangers, locksmiths would be out of work. We would have no wish to screen our children's friends.

Fear of death and strangers is our natural protection against premature travel to a better world. Love of our own, rotten world allows fear to put us on the alert. Back when we were swinging from limb to limb in the Garden of Eden,[1] those sweaty palms required us to tighten our grips and start really discriminating between friendly and dangerous strangers lest we perish. Today the politically correct have elevated this natural fear of strangers into a mental illness.

A phobia is a fear, a social anxiety if you will. The DSM-5 (the fifth manual of mental illnesses voted most likely to succeed for insurance reimbursement) provides the code 300.23 for phobia or social anxiety. Fear of dropping a bar of soap in a prison shower room is diagnosed as "homophobia." Fear of hiring an idiot to do a moron's job is diagnosed as "idiot-phobia." And if you are afraid of hiring a nanny for your children just because he is a stranger without references and you are concerned with the "pedophilia rocks" tattoo divided between his buttocks and peeking over his beltline, then you have a fear of strangers—better diagnosed as *xenophobia*. If you need more digits for reimbursement, look them up yourself. Sadly, xenophobia will hardly guarantee you a job under the Americans with Disabilities Act. Nor will it shield you from the thought police.

Unlike dyslexia, which could at least earn you extra time on your Scholastic Aptitude Test, xenophobia merely qualifies as one of Bill Moyers's seven deadly sins. To review: racism, sexism, nativism, homophobia, xenophobia, intolerance, and conservative hate speech. The condition is merely an excuse to toss us into Hillary Clinton's "basket of deplorables" to remove our voices from the political fray. (Not that we need any excuse to be deplorable and proud.)

IRRATIONAL FEAR OR COMMON SENSE?

As xenophobia's rejection by PC suggests, the condition is nothing but common sense. The phobia inspires us to hand out nanny positions and green cards with caution. No one who could have passed the Ellis Island health and intelligence tests would be stupid enough to hire someone without a job interview and reference check. The same cautions that apply to entering into relationships in general apply in diamonds to entering into time-consuming, income-producing relationships with strangers.

Take, for instance, breaking into the New York publishing industry.

Before the Internet and self-publishing, New York publishing enjoyed quite the monopoly on what books were admitted into the culture. Many individuals joined the publishing community, not for a love of money (there wasn't much, considering talent; one could easily make more as a stockbroker, lawyer, or doctor) but a love of books and of filtering the relationships between writers and readers.

Being created in God's image won't get you hired as an editor. Publishers severely discount God's image as a stamp of approval. Instead publishers require that editors first be examined by the university system—a relationship such as a personal introduction from a colleague of the publisher or the privilege of graduating from an Ivy League school not necessarily being an impediment to being hired.

Having gone through the decade-and-a-half vetting process that began in kindergarten and could continue for decades more of career advancement, the editor is trained by example to discriminate between author applicants. Strangers need not apply. Most editors limit their relationships to communication with literary agents. To get within a New York mile of a New York literary agent, you need a letter of recommendation from God or, better yet, celebrity status or a hefty social media platform. The way to not be a stranger is to not be a stranger in the first place, having already made a name for yourself.

HOW TO BREAK IN (POLITELY)?

I remember in the early 1990s, when I resolved to break into publishing, I bought a copy of Jeff Herman's *Writers Guide*, studied it carefully, and sent out what seemed like a hundred queries. In return, I received a hundred "Dear Author" form-letter rejections. I seriously considered changing my name to "Author" so I could boast a personal relationship with an agent.

Eventually things changed. Back then, there were no digital piles, just paper. In a literary agency, the daily stacks of incoming query letters were a foot high. I decided to make the stack even higher. Along with my query letter, I sent a two-pound box of Godiva chocolate. In return, I received a rejection from the Jane Dystel Literary Agency. It was addressed to Dr. Cook.

I was no longer a stranger. The agency subsequently sold a different book proposal of mine, this time for *Visual Fitness: 7 Minutes a Day to Better Eyesight and Beyond,* to Berkeley Books.

The point here is not that New York literary folk, because of their treatment of strangers, belong with those of us with good sense in the "basket of deplorables." Saying hello with a smile and a sincere hope for a stranger's good fortune is one thing. Inviting a stranger into a serious and costly relationship that could well determine the future direction of your life is quite another. I went through a twenty-year vetting process—known as education—to prove I had the persistence necessary to become an optometrist. In my residency at the State University of New York, I met practically everyone who was anyone in vision therapy, my chosen specialty in the profession. Within a few years, I was publishing papers, lecturing across America, and writing questions for the National Board of Examiners in Optometry. I was no longer a stranger. I had paid my dues.

As any editor or agent knows, time is money. Any time devoted to one person is no longer available to devote to another. The time an agent allots to a writer, if all goes well for both writer and agent, will correlate with the size of book royalties and commission checks. Strangers may or may not kill you, but the odds predict they are very likely to kill your time. Sure, every life has equal worth, but when it comes to playing the game of life, not everyone has equal value. Before we invite people into a time-consuming, possibly life-changing relationship, we invite those strangers to pay their dues.

In fraternities and sororities, there is hazing. In law firms, there are ungodly hours. In love affairs, no one but a rapist gets to home plate without running the bases—and that can be tough when strangers are not even admitted into the stadium.

In the case of immigration, the rules do not change. Those who come to America have seldom been welcomed by the citizenry en masse. The Kennedys were hardly royalty when they got off the ship from Ireland—even though they eventually came about as close to royalty as America allows, with a little help from Prohibition and bootlegging.

Getting my wife here from Vietnam took work. Paperwork, paperwork, paperwork. I consulted a lawyer. I kept complete documentation of my eight trips to Vietnam as well as a year and a half of daily phone calls, lest we needed to prove that we had a genuine relationship and that I was not merely being paid to pose as a fiancé to fool immigration. When she passed her interview at the American Consulate in Vietnam, we flew to America and lived in sin for a week before the judge, according to Georgia law, demanded we commit until "death do you part." Fortunately, my wife didn't understand English, so she hardly knew what she was promising. I took advantage of the opportunity, you could say.

Over the next few years, she not only learned English, she memorized the hundreds of questions that might appear on her interview to become a citizen. We listened to the questions whenever we were in the car. Do you know how many congressmen there are? My wife did. Overall, it took her four or five years to secure the visas, the green cards, and the United States citizenship. She paid her dues.

If she had been politically correct, she could have walked over the border of a country in which we are not equal under the law, a country with one set of rules for Hispanics and another set for Asians, Africans, and Europeans—not to mention other groups that will remain nameless.[2] But then politically correct, open borders have not won out—for the present.

America does not have nearly the good sense about strangers held by other countries. My wife has two cousins from Vietnam who obtained student visas to study in Australia. One studied fashion design, the other accounting. When it came time to apply for Australian citizenship, the accountant got in. The fashion designer was informed that he would be of no benefit to Australia. To receive his citizenship, he retrained as an accountant and got in.

To paraphrase President Kennedy's inaugural speech, "Ask not what our country can do for strangers. Ask what strangers can do for our country." And admit them on that basis.

This is just common sense when committing to a relationship with a stranger. Sure, sleep with your front door left open if your heart is bigger than your mind. If you want that psychotic drunk freezing in the gutter to be free to immigrate into your home, good for you. You're a saint. But if your wife has any sense, she'll insist that the undocumented alien wet *your* side of the bed. During your quest for heightened exploration that comes with the novelty of diversity, she'll let you contend with the snot in the psychotic's beard.

Before we end, let me confess why I am deplorable and proud. I am a xenophobe. I am proud to admit that I sleep with the door not only closed, but locked. If I had children, I would not hire a nanny off a raffle; I would insist on a job interview and references. I would want to know my children's friends so I could screen for potential harm. I think xenophobia is nothing but a demand for safe borders, nothing but common sense. But then don't trust me: I'm a stranger. I could be merely justifying my own deplorability.

The next time a fool accuses you of xenophobia, thank him for the praise and for acknowledging your wisdom. Be proud that you are not a politically correct idiot. Recommend the drunk on the local park bench to tutor your accuser's daughter. This will tell you if your accuser is really a politically correct fool or just an out-and-out hypocrite. Hire a locksmith to remove the locks from your accuser's house. Leave his front door standing open. Then see who's afraid of strangers. The New Moral Majority (NMM) tell us that xenophobia is not only immoral but in poor taste. If your accuser fails the taste test, invite him to join us in becoming deplorable and proud.

NATIVISM

While xenophobia revolves around fear, nativism revolves around competition for making a living. The Oxy Morons, shining across the shining sea, define this peculiarly United States term as "The policy of protecting the interests of native-born or established inhabitants against those of immigrants." Nativism, it turns out, is but one more of the revised seven deadly sins, those macro-transgressions magnified from the micro-morality of the NMM.

As any patron of PC could tell us, nativism is an evil ism, ranking up there with sexism and racism. Despite the poet Robert Frost's wisdom that "good fences make good neighbors," open borders are obviously tempting. Turning Europe into a Trojan horse will prove once and for all the efficacy of open borders on halting or spreading terrorism. We can see how the experiment works before deciding on our own immigration policy.

In the meantime, we can thank those who first welcomed us to these shores. Luckily for us, the Native Americans in their native bliss were not nativists. Favoring inclusion, and understanding full well that borders are made by people in opposition to natural law, they were happy to share the continent with their European American brothers and sisters and were blessed many times over for their freedom from irrational phobias about competition from immigrants.

And we killed those who had any doubts.

Nativism is nothing new, having pretty much always been the American way. In 1790, the First Congress passed "An act to establish an uniform rule of Naturalization." The act opened citizenship to any "free white person, who shall have resided within the limits and under the jurisdiction of the United States for the term of two years ..." providing, of course that "he is a person of good character." The children of such a person would automatically become citizens, except "that the right of citizenship shall not descend to persons whose fathers have never been resident in the United States."

Thus, pretty much from the get-go of America, exclusionism was already thriving. White and black slaves, and blacks, and underage bastards residing here with their mothers rather than their fathers—who still lived on foreign soil—were excluded, at least until maturity, from citizenship. So far, so good.

By 1795, the United States was growing more exclusive, the "uniform rule of Naturalization" of that year extending required residency to five years. "A person of good character" was no longer good enough for America. Now "good moral character" was required, which, if enforced, would have barred most of humanity from our political body. The United States would have been as empty as heaven without God's grace. Luckily, however, evil thoughts were hard to count, so the clause was never strictly interpreted or enforced. Still, would-be citizens were required to renounce any "hereditary title" or "order of nobility," not to mention any "allegiance and fidelity to any foreign prince, potentate, state, or sovereignty." Having barred any trace of nobility from our citizenry, exclusionism was advancing.

In 1798, nativism made a quantum leap. The English and French were at war (so what's new?) and siding with the English rather than the French (always a good idea!), the Fifth Congress amended the "uniform rule of naturalization" to require new residents to have "resided within the United States fourteen years, at least," before becoming citizens. The statute also provided that "no alien, who shall be a native, citizen, denizen or subject of any nation or state with whom the United States shall be at war, at the time of his application, shall be then admitted to become a citizen of the United States."

In 1800, the renowned racist and sexist Thomas Jefferson stuck a blow to exclusionism, returning to the required five years of residency for those wishing to become citizens. Despite some unsuccessful attempts to ban Catholics, progress in exclusion and nativism slowed until 1875. Then America really got serious about quality control in immigration. At that time, the Forty-Third Congress passed the Page Law, which stated the following:

Sec. 3. That the importation into the United States of women for the purposes of prostitution is hereby forbidden; and all contracts and agreements in relation thereto, made in advance or in pursuance of such illegal importation and purposes, are hereby declared void; and whoever shall knowingly and willfully import, or cause any importation of, women into the United States for the purposes of prostitution, or shall knowingly or willfully hold, or attempt to hold, any woman to such purposes, in pursuance of such illegal importation and contract or agreement, shall be deemed guilty of a felony, and on conviction thereof, shall be imprisoned not exceeding five years and pay a fine not exceeding five thousand dollars.

The statute was of course sexist, ignoring male prostitutes, but nevertheless barred "obnoxious persons," which, if PC were in force, would have included the deplorable and proud. For our purposes, however, we see that protecting American prostitutes from undue competition was the purpose of the bill. Thank God and Uncle Sam for nativism.

Over the next few decades, the U.S. Congress took care of the "coolie trade" and handled "peons," but in 1917 the Sixty-Fourth Congress really gave nativism a boost, barring "idiots, imbeciles, feeble-minded persons, . . . insane persons; . . . persons of constitutional psychopathic inferiority; . . . paupers; professional beggars; vagrants," etc. In short—the politically correct and those they now champion. Add these to those "obnoxious persons" (conservatives?) mentioned in 1875, and the law could have been cited to give America back to the natives that the European Americans, my forebears, stole it from in the first place. More importantly, though, and certainly more germane to our chapter, the 1917 act again protected our domestic skin trade with the following exclusions:

Sec. 3 . . . Prostitutes, or persons coming into the United States for the purpose of prostitution or for any other immoral purpose; persons who directly or indirectly procure or attempt to procure or import prostitutes or persons for the purpose of prostitution or for any other immoral purpose; persons who are supported by or receive in whole or in part the proceeds of prostitution . . .

Male prostitutes were now covered by the law, but other than that, what has nativism accomplished for America? According to the Statistic Brain,[3] the average annual income of a U.S. prostitute is $290,000. By contrast, lawyers prostitute themselves for an average of only $129,000.[4] The oldest profession, it seems, owes its prosperity to nativism thwarting the boom in human trafficking. The obvious solution to the inequality in earning potential is to open the borders to prostitutes and close the borders to the human trafficking of lawyers. In this manner, members of the legal profession will soon make enough not to have to moonlight as politicians. The prostitutes, now suffering from international competition but untainted by legal ethics, could supplement their incomes as politicians to the moral benefit of the nation.

Despite the moralizing of the NMM, perhaps some nativism is more equal than others.

CHAPTER 12

VIEWPOINTS ON RACISM: PAINTING POLITICS BY THE QUOTAS[1]

Maybe it's time to scrap the world "racist." Find something new. Like Racial Disorder Syndrome. And we could have different categories for sufferers of the syndrome: mild, medium, and acute.

—*Chimamanda Ngozi Adichie*

RACE

The most astonishing discovery provided by a thorough exploration into the peculiarities of race is the extreme feebleness of European blood. The primary evidence for this deficiency appears in Virginia's Racial Integrity Act of 1924:

Be it enacted by the General Assembly of Virginia . . . It shall hereafter be unlawful for any white person in this State to marry any save a white person.... For the purpose of this act, the term "white person" shall apply only to the person who has no trace whatsoever of any blood other than Caucasian....

Adults, on average, have something between a gallon and a gallon and a half of blood—depending on how much room is left over by alcohol content. According to legislative wisdom it takes only "one drop" of dark blood to stain the contents of an entire European circulatory system—heart, arteries, capillaries, and veins. We can sensibly conclude that the feebleness of European blood is second only to the foolishness of lawmakers' imaginations.

It gets even more bizarre. The hypocrisy of Enlightenment politics promised us that "all men are created equal." The sentiment created problems. How could we excuse slavery? How could we justify European imperialism exploiting the resources of the non-white globe? Luckily, the Enlightenment smoothed the inconsistency of logic by bequeathing us modern science.

The most famous science book of the nineteenth century was Charles Darwin's *On the Origin of Species by Means of Natural Selection, or the Preservation of Favoured Races in the Struggle for Life.* To reconcile Darwin's title with the Enlightenment principle of equality required science to divide the human race into smaller "races" or the human species into "subspecies" and then claim that some of these divisions should be better preserved and favored than others. Humanity, especially when running in political or social-scientific packs, is prone to disappoint. Separating the human race into distinct black, white, red, and yellow races was about as successful as trying to separate the wheat from the chaff in a fallow field.

As long as politics demanded the concept of *race*, science continued to dissect the human race into smaller disappointments. But then political correctness (PC) came along to turn "race" into an embarrassment, failing to mesh with the movement's delusion of equality. Once more, politics turned to the science that had provided the blessing of eugenics, and would soon predict the perils of climate change, and asked for help. Recombining all those races back into the human race would, once more, allow equality.

Happily, the metaphors of science are exquisitely fluid, science being best defined as "the art of arranging observations to fit theory."[2] As "Darwin's Bulldog," Thomas Henry Huxley, wrote, "In the ultimate analysis everything is incomprehensible, and the whole object of science is simply to reduce the fundamental incomprehensibilities to the smallest possible number."[3] In science, dozens of definitions compete to capture both "life" and "species" with no sign of any definitive winner in the fray.[4] Attempts to reduce "life" into "species" and "species" into "subspecies" or "race" are about as successful as neuro-astrology predicting our fates by reading the constellations of our brain cells.

To keep the politicians happy, scientists can, however, agree that genetically speaking it is impossible to tell where one "race" begins and another ends. Fish and whales gotta swim and bats and birds gotta fly, but similarity of appearance and function are no clue to similarity of genetics. Whose genes most resemble those of Africans, Australian aborigines or Scandinavians? Is skin color or the length of the hike from Africa the better predictor of genetic diversity? Scientists can similarly shuffle the deck of genes to provide evidence of more differences within a "race" than between "races." Today both "race" and Pluto's planethood have lost the vote of scientific consensus—until the next election, anyway.

Distinguished university professor and research geneticist Daniel J. Fairbanks writes in his book *Everyone Is African: How Science Explodes the Myth of Race:*

> Racial classification is real, but it is based much more on a set of social definitions than on genetic distinctions. Legally defined categories for race differ from one country to another, and they change over time depending largely on the social and political realities of a particular society or nation. The notion of discrete racial categories arose mostly as an artifact of centuries-long immigration history coupled with overriding worldview that white superiority was inherent—a purported genetic destiny that has no basis in modern science.[5]

There we have it right from the gene expert's mouth:[6] "race" is groupthink, not biology. Don't blame the biologists who sold the think for most of two hundred years. Don't blame Darwin for inadvertently providing the inspiration that Hitler needed to justify killing six million human beings for daring to belong to the wrong "race." Race is in our minds, not our genes. Biology and genetics have little to do with it. One thing is for sure, if race is a concept constructed by the human race, then it's bound to be as imaginatively perverse as we are.

SKIN-THINK

Race—damned if we use the term, damned if we don't. If race is real, seams divide our biological equality. If race is not real, neither is our excuse for seeking political redress for the grievances of ancestors forever lost to all but memory, imagination, and the thirst for restitution. The trick, it seems, is to maintain that we are exactly equal, but that when it comes to politics some of us are more exactly equal than others.

Because the words *race* and *color* are emotionally charged, shattering any hope of reason, I suggest that, in the tradition of political correctness, we come up with a less emotion-laden term, a euphemism burying the travails of the past, at least until their ghosts resurface to labor in the present. In our case, since race is little more than groupthink about skin, why not replace *race* with the euphemism *skin-think?*

Skin-think easily covers brown faces, red necks, and gleaming shaved heads. Although skin-think lacks the emotional punch needed for selling ideologies, we can always save *racism* for when we require emotion to confuse the reason of our political rivals. As David Hollinger, the Preston Hotchkis Professor of History emeritus at the University of California, Berkeley, assures us, "Racism is real, but races are not."

Kind of like sexism without sex, Buddhism without Buddha, and liberalism without PC.

RACISM

Is the principal evil of racism in the *ism* or in the violence and terror—two commodities that transcend race? Would Jeffrey Dahmer's cannibalism have been more repulsive if he had preferred white meat to dark? Would he have been a better person if he had included more Hispanics or Native Americans in his diet?

As I discussed this chapter with a friend, he admonished me, "If you were black, then you would understand the meaning of racism." I was chastened, at least until I bothered to think. How much better do Will Smith, Morgan Freeman, Oprah Winfrey, and President Obama understand the meaning of racism than I do? Do they lose sleep over some honky in Birmingham or Atlanta using skin-think to justify his imagined superiority? Nothing has really changed with those who ride their industry and talent rather than their race. More than a hundred years ago, former slave Booker T. Washington wrote from the perspective of one who could see past race:

> There is another class of coloured people who make a business of keeping the troubles, the wrongs, and the hardships of the Negro race before the public. Having learned that they are able to make a living out of their troubles, they have grown into the settled habit of advertising their wrongs—partly because they want sympathy and partly because it pays. Some of these people do not want the Negro to lose his grievances, because they do not want to lose their jobs.[7]

Victimization requires the consent of the victimized. Washington refused to give that consent, refused to hate. He understood, perhaps, that his own education and success were the best revenge, that the key to his own life was in his own hands, not the hands of his oppressors. He transcended race to write, "I would permit no man, no matter what his colour might be, to narrow and degrade my soul by making me hate him."[8] He understood the poison of power—the treatment of the powerless by the powerful, the spreading hatred of each for the other—and wrote, "The white man who begins by cheating a Negro usually ends up by cheating a white man. The white man who begins to break the law by lynching a Negro soon yields to the temptation to lynch a white man."[9] Washington saw past race to view humanity, understood that sin's power was blind to race. He was no racist, no champion of race; he was a champion of humanity.

Except for political or economic battles, is it really necessary to subdivide man's inhumanity toward man by color? Do our dancing skills really matter when we come to the ends of our ropes? Does skin-think make lives matter more? Are human rights exceeded by rights justified by skin-think? Is the Golden Rule more golden if it includes a postscript on skin? Which would you prefer: being the victim of racial preference, violence, or homicide? If you found yourself walking on an unfriendly block, which would you prefer: life or love? Would you prefer affronts to your soul or your body, jeers or bullets?

We will return to such questions, but for now the most difficult problem with racism may not be racism itself but exactly how to define the word, for depending on the definition we use, racism is or is not an equal opportunity employer. During the remainder of this chapter, we will, therefore, struggle with the problems of any simple definition for *racism*, and then offer one: *skin-think justification*. Racism uses skin-think to *justify violating individuals in order to alter or preserve the economic, political, or social status quo*. Find skin-think; find an excuse; find a racist: exploiting, terrorizing, violating, denying, libeling, slandering, dehumanizing, demeaning, boycotting, or silencing.

CUTTING NATURE AT ITS JOINTS

In exploring definitions for racism, let's begin closer to the beginning, going back a couple of thousand years. As we discussed in a footnote in our first chapter, according to Socrates, who was executed for being politically incorrect, some words, such as *gold*, "cut nature at its joints." Pure gold gives us a solid boundary with gold on one side and silver, lead, and hogwash on the other. If eleven knowledgeable men and one divinely beautiful woman discuss gold, they will all agree on the nature of the element that will shortly end up resting on the woman's ring finger.

If the same dozen participants explore the word *love*, which all imagine to rumble in their hearts, agreement will give way to a diversity of opinions: love means cherishing; love means being a soulmate; love means taking out the trash; love means the sweetness of lips or the bulge of the bank account, the glitter of the kiss or diamond. Love means training your husband to beg with the same kindness and persistence you use to train the dog; love means crediting your husband for the invention of the ideas he stole from you; love means never having to say you're sorry, because it goes without saying you will be before your wife starts talking to you again. Etc.

Only after the dozen love explorers have thrown all these observations and opinions into the blender of groupthink will they come up with a definition upon which none can really agree but all can accept. The definition of love will not cut nature at the joints even though you might imagine that the lucky gentleman with the gold, who won the competition for the hand of the beautiful woman, is a bilateral amputee from how much time he spends on his knees, begging. The definition of love, however unnatural it is, allows, as Socrates in Plato's

Phaedrus argues, "speech to proceed clearly and consistently with itself." Which means that the woman's desires come first if the desires of the man are to come at all.

So, is the word *racism* like love or gold? Does it cut nature at the joints, or does it consist of diverse opinions voted in by groupthink and certain to provoke debate? Or rather, would the term *racism* provoke debate were it not for the threat of PC sentencing one debate team to share Socrates' hemlock?

RACISM AT OXFORD

According to the Oxy Morons,[10] racism may be defined as "(Belief in, adherence to, or advocacy of) the theory that *all* members of each race possess characteristics, abilities, qualities, etc., specific to that race, esp. distinguishing it as inferior or superior to another race or races; prejudice, discrimination, or antagonism based on this."

Is this definition as sound as gold or merely politically correct noise? Is this *racism* an editorial committee's vote to present PC as truth? The morons admit that racism revolves around belief in a theory. Nevertheless, the terms *racism* and *love* share a failure to cut nature at the joints even though both are often used to bring people to their knees.

According to the Oxy Morons' definition, for example, physicians are all racists, treating whites and African Americans as if they belong to different bell curves. Physicians assume that sickle cell anemia is more prevalent with Africans than Scandinavians. As we noted in chapter one, the bell curve is the scientific name for prejudice. The curve invites us to prejudge people. As any doctor worth his salt knows, however, we examine persons, not bell curves.

Actually, I lied. Physicians' thinking on sickle cell anemia is not racism, the key word in the Oxy-Moronic definition being *all*. By definition, we are not racists unless we prejudge *all* Africans to have sickle cell anemia. Thus, physicians escape the definition of racism, at least on this count.

The *all* rule can similarly be applied in evaluating the case of James Watson, who in 1962 shared the Nobel Prize for the most significant biological discovery in the twentieth century, the structure of DNA. In 2007, Watson, still hung over from his Darwinian binge on editing *Darwin: The Indelible Stamp*, explained during a *Sunday Times Magazine*[11] interview that "there is no firm reason to anticipate that the intellectual capacities of peoples geographically separated in their evolution should prove to have evolved identically. Our wanting to reserve equal powers of reason as some universal heritage of humanity will not be enough to make it so." Watson also confessed that he was "inherently gloomy about the prospect of Africa" because "All our social policies are based on the fact that their intelligence is the same as ours—whereas all the testing says not really."

Suffering the terrorist attacks of the politically correct, Watson promptly lost his job and later ended up selling his Nobel medal to cope with the reduced circumstances of his income and social status. But is Watson a racist? According to the Oxy Morons, he is not. In the same interview that precipitated his banishment, Watson said, "There are many people of colour who are very talented, but don't promote them when they haven't succeeded at the lower level." Thus Watson—although not cheery about the affirmative action that has called into question the competence of truly gifted human beings being confused for those who rose according

LAUGHING AT POLITICAL CORRECTNESS

to political privilege rather than merit—did not meet the *all* criteria of racism. He did fail the more stringent requirements of PC. He made negative comments about members of a "particular" group.

Any of us who would agree that President Obama is a brilliant rhetorician would, like Watson, escape being dubbed racists under the *all* provision provided by the Oxy Morons. Similarly, if we believe the universal superiority of African Americans as dancers and athletes, we are racists. If we accept superior dancing and athletics as rules of thumb, not foot, then again, we are not, according to the Oxy Morons, racists.

What's going on here? Did the Oxy Morons get the definition wrong? In *New York Times Magazine,* an article appeared, "The Easiest Way to Get Rid of Racism? Just Redefine It."[12] The article examined those who suggest that if we reduce racism to malice in the heart, then anyone who favors one race over another, whether white supremacist or affirmative action advocate, could be a racist.

If logic is to prevail, the article gets it right, but perhaps the article still misses the point. Maybe the confusion rests in stretching one little term to cover both a murder and a joke. Maybe the confusion rests in what happens when we make up definitions of a term that do not cut nature at the joints. Anyone can take out a butcher knife and block and have at it. Racism becomes whatever we want it to be to defeat our political enemies and command the sway of the world. The term is incoherent, like a one-way street in which the flow of traffic is determined by thought. Since PC forbids us to share our thoughts, collisions just keep occurring. No one seems to know where they, or anyone else, is headed. Is racism hatred evoked by the color of one's skin or laughter evoked by the color of one's remarks?

How do we best butcher a term that does not cut nature at the joints? Perhaps examining the term from a number of viewpoints will help.

Or not.

THE LESS-IS-MORE VIEWPOINT OF RACISM

The word *misanthrope* is derived from the Greek *miso* and *anthrōpos*. *Miso* comes from the base *misein* meaning "to hate." *Anthrōpos* means "man" or "mankind." Racism is the theory that hating a part of mankind is worse than hating all of mankind. Misanthropes did not make it into Hillary Clinton's "basket of deplorables" or Bill Moyers's revised version of the seven deadly sins. According to political correctness, misanthropy is not heresy. Hating everyone (especially straight, conservative Christian men) is perfectly okay. Indeed, it could be argued that some promotors of PC are actually disguised misanthropes just as were many of the inquisitors of the Spanish Inquisition.

The evidence suggests, however, that it is safer to hate all than some. Imagine someone calling you a "misanthrope." You and the room would probably yawn, experiencing no notable alarm. If, however, someone were to call you a "racist," you would tremble in your boots, fearing for your livelihood. Such are the terror tactics of PC.

THE OTHER-RACE VIEWPOINT ON RACISM

We could say that racists are those who commit harmful acts against members of other races, but not against their own race. If, for instance, a white supremacist bullies, intimidates, or assaults white people standing up for blacks, the supremacist is not a racist. He treats members of both races violently and cruelly; he is merely antisocial (a full-blooded, man-and-woman-hating misanthrope, if you will). Similarly, if some young African American shoots and steals from an African American shop owner and hates the white police officers who arrest him, he hardly qualifies as a racist. He is just filled with hate and lack of respect for human life and property. Like the supremacist, he is merely another antisocial hiding behind his skin.

In the movie *The Help*, Ronnie Howard's daughter, Bryce Dallas Howard, plays the role of Hilly. Hilly provides us with a case study of a psychopath. She intimidates not just African Americans but everyone in the film. She brings out the worst in everyone, even the audience. When one of her victims feeds Hilly human feces disguised as chocolate pie, we inhumanely applaud the less than appetizing act. Hilly's rage evokes our own. Her seething hatred gives the movie its motive force. Without her social road rage, there would be no movie. What's important to note is that Hilly sees the whole world as potential enemies threatening her imagined position of superiority. She is an equal opportunity bully. She is a racist in the strongest sense of the word; she hates the human race.

The question arises, how many people naturally exhibit hatred around one skin color but feel only love around creatures of their own skin color? Or does the relative defenselessness of minorities just allow sociopaths to exhibit their inhumanity as they secretly rage against all whom they imagine to contest their fantasized superiority? Is a blow against race nothing more or less than a blow against mankind?

THE LOVE VIEWPOINT ON RACISM

Are we racists if we love too much? Suppose we love our own children more than we love the actress Zoe Saldana in the role of the green-skinned assassin Gomora in *Guardians of the Galaxy*. Does this make us racists against green aliens? Suppose we love our children and those who most resemble them more than we love Saldana when she is blue-skinned in *Avatar* or dark skinned in *Star Trek*?[13] Does this expand our green-skinned racism to blue or black skin? If we love blonds more than brunettes are we automatically colorists? Does too much love for one group compared to another group similarly make us racists? If we love those who look like our families more than those who do not, are we racists? Is racism about unequal love or hate and violence?

THE DEHUMANIZATION VIEWPOINT ON RACISM

Mark Twain assured us, "Man is the only animal that blushes. Or needs to." If all humans blush, then those beings that reportedly do not blush, or cannot be reported to blush, are not human. Thus, paradoxically, demanding that we not mention the blushing of particular groups is to demand we portray the members of that exact group as "blush free"; that is, not human.

Many would agree that racism is an attempt to dehumanize a person. Once a person's humanity has been stolen or sufficiently questioned, then it is possible to persecute him. If we pretend that green people are not human, it makes it okay to vilify or mistreat green people. No differently, if we imagine that racists, sexists, nativists, homophobes, xenophobes, and conservatives unafraid to speak their minds are, because of their beliefs, not human, then it makes it okay to vilify and mistreat them. In the same way, if we pretend that someone is sinless, we dehumanize him. To claim that all green people are without sin is racism because the claim dehumanizes green people.

THE MATHEMATICAL-LOGIC VIEWPOINT ON RACISM

Is racism in the numbers, not the intent; the math, not the hatred? Consider an example. If once upon a time an Asian gentleman living in Japan considered white visitors to be barbarians, then the gentleman, being a part of the majority, was a racist. If this same gentleman were to immigrate to America and maintained the identical views on the inferiority of barbarian whites, then despite the exact same arrogance, prejudice, and hate, now being in the minority, he would no longer be a racist. Seem logical? In this view, racism depends neither on our prejudices or petty hatreds; it depends on the relative size of our group. The easiest way to eliminate racism in America would be to reduce whites to another minority. Make sense?

Similarly, if European Americans were to vote as a bloc on issues affecting African Americans, would they qualify as racists? Would African Americans bloc voting on the same issues not qualify as racists unless their numbers tipped the balance of the scale? Is racism about belief or census taking? If some European American imagines himself to be superior to all other Americans, is he a racist? If some Native American imagines himself to be superior to European Americans, is he a racist? Is all supremacism racism, or just white supremacism? Or is adding the "white" to supremacism just racism? Are green and purple supremacists okay—so long as they are in the minority? Is only majority supremacism supremely evil?

THE WORDS-VERSUS-ACTIONS VIEWPOINT ON RACISM

Is racism about words, the stories we tell ourselves and others, and not our actions? Take the case of Donald Sterling, former owner of the Los Angeles Clippers basketball franchise. During a spat[14] with his girl (we won't call her a "girlfriend" because she didn't sound much like a "friend" as she cross-examined him, repeatedly baiting him to reveal his views on race). Sterling, whose family was involved in a lawsuit alleging that Sterling's young companion had embezzled 1.8 million dollars, dutifully confessed, "There's nothing wrong with minorities, they're fabulous." "I love the black people." "I've known him [Magic Johnson] well and he should be admired."

Sure, one could imagine a certain irony in Sterling's voice as he made some of these confessions, but Sterling was obviously too old to understand that in the digital world privacy has died along with freedom of thought. The conversation was conveniently being recorded. By whom? We can't say.

Sterling's comments in support of African Americans never passed the filters of the liberal press. Instead, Sterling's companion finally got him angry and jealous enough to blurt out, "It bothers me a lot that you want to broadcast that you're associated with black people. Do you have to?" and "Don't put him [Magic Johnson] on an Instagram for the world to have to see so they have to call me. And don't bring him to my games." Sterling's use of the words "black people" rather than "blacks" or "African Americans" stresses that he comes from a different generation or he sees African Americans not as abstractions but as human beings—rivals for the attention of his girlfriend, perhaps, but human beings.

What had most likely happened was that one of Sterling's old buddies, still stuck in an earlier, no longer fashionable era, had called him and provoked him, probably even making him the butt of a joke. His true love had only to stir the fire.

Sterling's alleged Alzheimer's disease may have been acting up that day because a later press release stated, "Mr. Sterling is emphatic that what is reflected on that recording is not consistent with, nor does it reflect his views, beliefs or feelings. It is the antithesis of who he is and what he believes and how he has lived his life."[15] The same could be true of any words taken out of the context of a life and posted on social media. With the terror of political correctness in the air, a single false word could destroy your life as completely as a single motorcycle accident.

If something untoward has ever come out of your mouth in a moment of anger, perhaps you can believe the Sterling press release, for the release was not out of line with his fifteen-to-twenty-year history of making so many contributions to the Los Angeles chapter of the NAACP that he won a lifetime achievement award in 2009 and was nominated for a second award in 2014. In the words of an NAACP spokesman, the award was for "a body of work. Mr. Sterling's organization has on a consistent basis brought in the minority community." His donations hardly characterized him as a hater of African Americans, at least those he didn't imagine were getting too close to the girl of his feeble affections and demented-fading fantasies.

Still, Sterling's actions were no insurance against the court of PC. Without a trial, he was convicted as a racist, denied his second NAACP award, deprived of his Clippers franchise, and banished from National Basketball Association games. Evidently, when it comes to PC, remarks made in anger are more important than decades of service. Racism in our words, not our actions, is close enough for politics.

JUSTIFICATION BY SKIN-THINK

What is justification? In their *Dictionary of Philosophy*, the Oxy Morons tell us an "action or belief is justified if it stands up to some kind of critical reflection or scrutiny; a person is then exempt from criticism on account of it."[16] In other words, justification is a sales pitch given to escape blame for a given belief or, perhaps, action. For sophists, behavioral scientists, and politicians, the proof of the pitch is in the sale. Philosophers demand the justification be backed by the rules of logic that always work, except for when they do not—valid arguments never proving anything absolutely.

Stories, if sold well enough to be believed, can trump action. Consider our firebombing of Dresden, Germany. The story that the terror and violence speeded the war's end, if believed, justifies the firestorm. The story of women and children screaming as they burned to death, if believed, could justify us as war criminals. But to the victors go the justifications. The single word *enemies* is often sufficient to justify homicide. Such is the power of justification. Our most potent weapon against justification is skepticism.

Racism, I argue, is skin-think justification—the use of skin-think for the purpose of justification. The definition plays no favorites. To justify hatred with skin-think is racism no matter what your race. Hate travels a two-way street. Hate is hate no matter how *particular* the direction. Avoiding one-way-street skin-think arguments allows us to avoid our earlier example of the wise old Japanese gentleman whose racism, but not fantasies of supremacism, change with the math of his *particular* majority or minority status.

Although the definition potentially doubles the size of the crop of racists, the definition also helps to differentiate. No racism occurs if a purple person loves his purple children more than he loves President Obama's black children, providing his love is justified by kinship or habitual closeness, not skin-think. If the love is justified by skin-think, then whoever supplies the justification is a racist, whether the purple father or a green accuser using skin-think to exclude the father from a political discussion.

As mentioned in chapter one, the best way to end discrimination is to curtail perception. A person who is truly color-blind will be conscious of skin-think no more than a person raised in a black-and-white world will be conscious of the color red. The color-blind have no understanding of skin-think justifications. Imagine a picture of a two-year-old European American child happily playing with an African American doll. The child, with perceptions yet to be developed, is color-blind. The photographer is not, using skin-think to justify a political faction adept at destroying the reputations and livelihoods of its rivals.

Skin-think justification is nothing new. Enlightenment-challenged Europeans employed skin-think to justify using their superior technical skills and achievements to subjugate the rest of the world. Rather than justifying slavery by its antiquity or that the great philosopher Aristotle wasted no words condemning slavery, American plantation owners used skin-think to justify slavery.[17] The Ku Klux Klan used skin-think to justify terrorism, brutality, and homicide. Law enforcement used skin-think to justify not uniformly enforcing laws to protect the life and property of its citizens. Scientists in Tuskegee, Alabama, used skin-think (not to mention the scientific method) to justify conducting experiments that allowed human beings to die of syphilis.[18] United States central government agencies such as the Federal Housing Administration used skin-think to justify granting or denying federally insured loans, thus dictating which citizens could afford to live in the suburbs. The list of how skin-think has been used to justify preserving the economic, political, and social status quo could fill volumes. Again, however, we must ask, was it the skin-think that was the sin or were the many perverse actions that skin-think was used to justify our real cause for concern?

Skin-think is also used to justify replacing, rather than preserving, the economic, political, or social status quo. How we justify the Civil War, for instance, helps to determine if we are racists. With no mention of skin-think we can justify the war as a continuation of the battle between the Federalists and Antifederalists, which began before the ratification of the Constitution—and continues to this very day. With no mention of skin-think, we can cite the abolishment of slavery to justify the war. The moment, however, we modify the word *slavery* with the words *African American*, then we are exploiting skin-think to help justify the deaths of 600,000 Americans—40,000 of them African American. We have become, per our definition, racists using skin-think to justify replacing the status quo.

Homicide is tragic, no matter the justification. "All lives matter" is uncommon sense and common decency—ask any mother of a slain child. "Black lives matter," while completely true, slights humanity by playing the skin-think card to justify political ends. Skin-think is similarly used to justify inequality in the quest for equality; affirmative action is a prime example of skin-think being used for justification. Using skin-think to justify awarding a job or premier university spot to one person rather than another is racism. Affirmative action is not, however, "reverse discrimination." Racism is racism; discrimination, discrimination. Skin-think justification has no direction, no need for one-way streets. We should all be equal under the law. Using skin-think to justify laws allowing some people to be more equal than others is just racism used to support politics.

How about using skin-think to justify razing statues? President George Washington was a heroic figure who held together the American Revolution. Without his inspiration there would probably be no United States of America. His contributions could easily justify raising his statue. However, George Washington was a white supremacist,[19] owning slaves for more than fifty years. Thus, skin-think can justify razing his statue. In the same way, skin-think can justify razing the statue of Robert E. Lee or any American who dreamed of manifest destiny or any Englishman who shaped the world during the time that the sun never set on the British Empire, or even the statue of Sir Isaac Newton, who changed the world with his science but owned stock in the East India Company and was thus a participant in the slave trade. Using skin-think to justify razing statues is, according to our definition, racism. It is just another example of using skin-think to justify changing the economic, political, and social status quo, another example of using skin-think to justify the dream of commanding the sway of the world.

RACISM REDUX

Picking up where we started and with what we missed, we earlier questioned if the sting of inhumanity was made worse by skin-think. We asked if the Golden Rule is made more golden by skin-think. We wondered if reducing human rights to Asian American, African American, and European American rights didn't just promote skin-think to justify political competition between special interest groups.

Skin-think provides neither an upgrade of the Golden Rule nor a justification for breaking it. Skin-think cannot modify the smart of our boo-boos, but justification may perpetuate or escalate the incidence of moral bumps and bruises. Skin-think is not the problem; words can't kill us but justified actions just might. As we've explored, the simple word *enemies* can justify a serial killer as a hero; the homicide and terror at Dresden were justified with one word: *war.* While the n-word has justified most every inhumanity known to man; the r-word has justified abridging our free speech and livelihoods. The problem is not the words: *war, nigger, enemies, supremacist,* or *racist.* The problem is our failure to be skeptical of justification used to explain away our humanity—or inhumanity. In truth, the only action skin-think justifies is scratching.

Another question: is all racism equal? Justifying a hanging is a far cry from justifying the laughter from a joke, but the damage created by scribbling the n-word on the wall of a building could be less damaging than posting the word *racist* on the wall of a Facebook business page.[20] Both words are forms of terrorism.

The word *racism,* because of its association with past violence, creates a gut reaction reducing from reason to passion all assessment of arguments of the word used in situations without violence. The words *skin-think justification* are neutral, allowing us to rationally compare the peeling of apples and oranges.

Is it evil to use skin-think justification to argue for equality under the law or freedom of speech or common decency or kindness toward all? Is it wrong to use skin-think justification to argue against hypocrisy or inhumanity or violence or terror or inequality under the law or laws, imagining that unequal treatment can ever equal equality? Perhaps not all examples of skin-think justification are the same. Perhaps in a world filled with skin, worldwide skin blindness is neither possible nor desirable. Perhaps we need to focus on precisely identifying what is being justified by the skin-think justification and accept or reject it accordingly. Arguments, whether for or against hangings and free speech, certainly need to be justified, but they cannot be justified by skin-think.

SUMMARY

Rather than cutting nature at the joints, the word *racism* is borrowed to cut the throats of political opponents, raise group rights above human rights, replace reason with passion, promote preferential love as preferential hate, place descent before country, confuse the distinction between words and actions, exploit the size and interests of special interest groups, and impose political handicaps against the winners of races. *Racism* is quite simply skin-think justification, skin-think justifying the violation of individual rights in order to alter or preserve the political, economic, or social status quo. Never fear to expose racism for the exact justification it is. Never make more of racism than what is being justified. And remember, justification can only harm when it's believed.

When recognizing justifications, begin with skepticism, throw out generalities, and, only after the most careful examination of the *particulars,* proceed to share in Mark Twain's pity "that Noah and his party did not miss the boat."

Even the Oxy Morons might now agree. By 2008 they had expanded their definition to include: "A belief that one's own racial or ethnic group is superior, or that other such groups represent a threat to one's cultural identity, racial integrity, or economic well-being."[21] While racism still relies on beliefs, not facts, we find no one-way-street definition here, no mention of "particular" groups. If red people and blue people are competing economically and see their competitors as a threat, they are racists. If they treasure diversity and don't want red and blue to be replaced by purple, they are racists. If the reds wear green hats and the blues wear yellow, then any movement toward black hats and white hats is racism. And, per our own definition, if color is used to justify ending, continuing, or altering any of these competitions, rivalries, imagined superiorities, or fashion trends, then once more we are looking at racism.

So, what is the solution to racism and blind prejudice? Blindness. Abolish perception. Worms have no eyes; not even PC accuses *them* of racism. Or we can take solace in the words of Jesus: "Therefore speak I to them in parables: because they seeing see not; and hearing they hear not, neither do they understand."[22] Understanding is obviously overrated. Having eyes and seeing not is probably as close as we'll come to an end of racism. Without perception, nobody discriminates.

CHAPTER 13

DENYING HISTORY—THE POLITICALLY CORRECT WAY

The very ink with which all history is written
is merely fluid prejudice.

—*Mark Twain*

Mark Twain also wrote, "If you tell the truth you don't have to remember anything." In other words, were it not for lies, historians would be out of work, having less to remember than politicians have to forget.

Formerly only historians could rewrite history, denying the past to repaint our imaginations about what actually happened. Then Darwin gave scientists the vote, allowing them to deny yesterday's histories as easily as tomorrow's discoveries will deny today's stories of science.

As I've commented elsewhere,[1] "For some, history is what happened. For many, history is a celebration of the events forming and unifying our culture. For the skeptic, history is a story told to reconcile the nightmares of yesterday with our dreams for tomorrow."

Twain's "fluid prejudice" captures the subject of history in two words. We all love denying history, recreating it to validate our passions. Unlike the Renaissance, during which the past vote on knowledge was treasured, today's prejudices are imagined to balance on the pinnacle of morality and truth. And yet what is the probability that our current groupthink will not itself topple under the weight of tomorrow's prejudices, creations, and discoveries?

All news becomes old news; old news is no news; no news is good news. Therefore, if we accept the premises, history is always good news—especially for those exploiting it to justify maintaining or changing the status quo. The possibilities for denying the fake news of history are endless, not so much because of what news made history as what news did not.

If, for instance, we examine the U.S. censuses from 1830, 40, 50, and 60, we can accurately report that the percentage of the population in slavery dropped from 15.6 percent to 14.5 percent to 13.8 percent to 12.6 percent. We can extrapolate (extend guesses about the past into guesses about the future) to argue that, without killing 600,000 Americans, slavery would have eventually petered out anyway, being replaced by technology rather than war. Such is the nature of rhetorical numbers and rhetorical reason.

Unfortunately, the census data also tell us that between 1830 and 1860 the number of slaves almost doubled, increasing from 2,009,043 to 3,953,761. Was slavery rising or decreasing? Both sets of statistics were true news, but context is all. Incomplete news, despite its accuracy or inaccuracy, is fake news. And fake news becomes fake history, just waiting to be denied.

FALSE POLITICAL ARGUMENTS

The stories of history are fascinating, so fascinating that they are excellent rhetorical tools for justifying our favorite political arguments. As always, the more detailed the historian's knowledge, the stronger the sales pitch. Just as in the mid fourteenth century astronomers used their intricate knowledge of the alignments of the heavens to explain "the great mortality," "black death," or "plague" that killed nearly half of Europe, and just as today neuroscientists use their intricate knowledge of the brain to explain reading problems or moral failings, those with a detailed knowledge of history can sell any political argument they care to sell—as I just used an historical analogy between astronomy-astrology and neurology-astrology to question historical arguments.

The historical argument I find most amusing is the two-wrongs-make-a-right argument, sometimes called the historical-scales-of-justice argument. Balancing the scales of justice between historical time periods is a bit like on Monday placing a brick on one platform of the scale, then on Friday moving the brick to the scale's other platform and claiming we have "balanced" the scales. Such historical justice typically rests more on politics than balance, more on revenge than justice. Still, history remains a powerful tool of persuasion. Those who cannot learn from the mistakes of the past are doomed not to make the sale in politics.

Excuse me if I have denied the value of historical arguments for other purposes than sales. Denying history is not without risk. In 1478 in Spain, denying the resurrection of Jesus Christ could have gotten you burnt at the stake. In 2017 in Spain, not to mention much of the European Union, denying the holocaust could get you thrown in jail—steel bars having surpassed charcoal-roasted stakes in popularity. History denial is not for the weak of heart, unless, for the sake of PC, we raise our trusty blue pencil to deny the history of an author's words that fall short of the virtues of our own golden age.

When it comes to words, history is another matter entirely. Tracing the history of a word is as risky as licking a dog's nose; you never know quite what it's been used for in the past. That acknowledged, the most famous denier of literary history is Thomas Bowdler (1754–1824). Bowdler, history tells us, was a physician, phenomenal chess player, and lover of Shakespeare's verse. Bowdler believed, though, that there was a problem with reading Shakespeare to those who were unequal to mature and discerning men such as Bowdler himself—in this case, meaning women. Bowdler, therefore, edited the bard to create *The Family Shakespeare in Three Volumes in which nothing is added to the original text; but those words and expressions are omitted which cannot with propriety be read aloud in a Family. The Dramatic Works of William Shakespeare adopted for Family Reading.*

Bowdler's justification for amputating feet from Shakespeare's verse provides an excellent study in condescension. Consider a section from Bowdler's preface:

It must, however, be acknowledged by his warmest admirers, that some defects are to be found in the writings of our immortal bard. The language is not always faultless. Many words and expressions occur which are of so indecent a nature as to render it highly desirable that they should be erased . . . and if these could be obliterated, the transcendent genius of the poet would undoubtedly shine with more unclouded lustre. To banish everything of this nature from his writings is the object of the present undertaking. It is the wish of the editor to render the plays of Shakespeare unsullied by any scene, by any speech, or, if possible, by *any word that can give pain to the most chaste, or offence to the most religious of his readers* [emphasis added].[2]

Bowdler did not want to chance "incurring the danger of [women and children] being hurt with any indelicacy of expression." Such censorship, with its purpose of avoiding "pain" or "offense," is always a tribute to the superior emotional and intellectual robustness of the censor compared to some supposedly inferior group—such as women, children,[3] or minorities. The withholding of information happily protects the "superior" and "inferior," keeping both in their natural places. The superiors maintain the power of information while the inferiors fail to mature, their sensitivities being heightened so that they can be easily overwhelmed and controlled by their emotions. Like Peter Pan's boys, the targeted group will not grow up. They'll never grow old. As any censor knows in his heart, keeping others weak is the ticket to elite power.

So how did Bowdler's censorship work? For one thing, he replaced the expletive "God" with the euphemism "Heavens"; "Good God!" simply became "Good Heavens!" While the euphemism hardly changes the sentiment, it simplifies things immensely. The word *God* is a bit difficult to wrap our finite minds around. God includes all that is so good that mortals can neither perceive nor imagine His goodness. Heaven is far simpler. Going to heaven is a little like having a tapeworm— you can eat all you want and not gain weight.

Still, Bowdler's use of euphemism helped prepare us for PC, for turning *secretary* into "executive assistant," *crippled* into "physically challenged," and *conservative* into "deplorable." In *Culture of Complaint*, Robert Hughes, an Australian-born art critic, writer, and producer of television documentaries, wrote about PC, "We want to create a sort of linguistic Lourdes, where evil and misfortune are dispelled by a dip in the waters of euphemism."[4]

Euphemism aside, Bowdler's greatest tool was to deny the existence of Shakespeare's words, kicking them out of history. In Act IV, Scene 5 of *Hamlet*, for instance, the Prince of Denmark's best girl, Ophelia, has flipped out after Hamlet has seemingly abandoned her, not to mention killing her father. She is, in the historical version of Shakespeare's play, singing bawdy songs in front of Hamlet's uncle, King Claudius:

OPHELIA   **Song**

> Tomorrow is Saint Valentine's day.
> All in the morning betime,
> And I a maid at your window
> To be your Valentine.
> Then up he rose and donned his clo'es
> And dupped* the chamber door, (*opened)
> Let in the maid, that out a maid
> Never departed more.

KING   **Pretty Ophelia!**
OPHELIA   Indeed without an oath, I'll make an end on't:
            By Gis and By Saint Charity,

> Alack, and fie for shame!
> Young men will do't if they come to't.
> By Cock, they are to blame.
> Quoth she, "Before you tumbled me,
> You promised me to wed."
> He answers:
> "So would I 'a' done by yonder sun,
> And thou hadst not come to my bed."
> KING   How long hath she been thus?

Bowdler's version denying the history of the movement of Shakespeare's pen:

OPHELIA   Good morrow, 'tis St. Valentine's day,
                    All in the morning betime,
                And I a maid at your window,
                    To be your Valentine.

KING   How long hath she been thus?

In the Bowdlerized version, the audience must wonder about the King's exclamation of concern about Ophelia's mentioning St. Valentine's day, but to protect those of us who, in Bowdler's mind, lack sophistication and powers of discrimination, he allows us to benefit from "reading Shakespeare" without being forced to read Shakespeare. Thus, riding on the arrogance of his imagined superiority, Bowdler allows a larger audience to pretend they are enjoying Shakespeare—not that aesthetically tailored histories are anything new; history is often being tailored to fit the rhetorical whims of the historian.

AND NEVER THE TWAIN WILL WE MEET

The spirit of Thomas Bowdler lives on. We are still being protected from the imagined preternatural power of words. I touched on this phenomenon in chapter two, where I lampooned "quack" as the "q-word."

While hyperbolic, these words are not untrue. When a culture "protects" us from words, that culture is actually sensitizing us so that the words, when used strategically, act as triggers to transport us into an irrational state—pretty much like stage hypnotism. One way to desensitize us to the words, if the intent is to disarm rather than arm the words, is to use them repeatedly, not turn them into taboos. Another way to disarm the word's power is to see the truth of the word.

In the case of the word *quack,* as I have written:

> Contemporary historian of science Frederick Gregory writes, "A quack in the German states of the eighteenth century was someone who poached on the territory and in so doing upset the proper economic order." The definition has not really changed. Like *scientific, quack* is still evoked primarily for the protection of economic turf.[5]

The same is true about the pejorative *nigger.* Used by the politically incorrect, the word is a weapon used to protect the status quo, to maintain the current economic, political, and social order. By the politically correct, the word is a weapon to overturn the current economic, political, and social order. By demonizing the word, we are merely increasing its emotional power. Both sides using the word sense this to be true at some level.

Playing into the hands of the lexical grenade makers, Twain scholar Alan Gribben has decided to deny history by expurgating[6] *Adventures of Huckleberry Finn*, removing the word *nigger*—all 215 uses of the epithet—from the text. The true history of the movement of Twain's pen be damned.

Gribben maintains that "the n-word remains inarguably the most inflammatory word in the English language." Who could argue with political correctness? Who could fail to argue that the n-word shocks more people than the f-word? And even if a few holdouts are more shocked by the f-word, at least Gribben, by removing the n-word from Huck's book, is doing what he can to empower the word as a hand grenade to destroy the enemy in the current social revolution.

Gribben, a professor of English at Auburn University, has devoted much of a lifetime of scholarship to Twain. Ironically, he argues that *Adventures of Huckleberry Finn* is about far more than Huck learning to see the runaway slave Jim as a human being:

> What Twain presents is a far more complex proposition—that it is conformist and cowardly of us to take it for granted that prevailing laws and customs, no matter how solidly established, are too sacred to be skeptically examined and intellectually tested by each of us individuals.[7]

Luckily, it is not conformist and cowardly to conform to cultural expectations when they demand altering 215 of

Twain's nouns and magnifying the shock value of the n-word because, as Gribben argues, "The American Library Association lists the novel among the most frequently challenged books across the nation" and because racial slurs "have increasingly presented a problem for teachers, students, and general readers." Evidently some "prevailing laws and customs" are more sacred than others.

Even more amusing is the denial of not only history but the plot of Twain's book. Like Bowdler reveling in the power of euphemisms, Gribben removes the word *nigger* and replaces it with the word *slave*. As Huck's dad says in Gribben's history-denying expurgated edition:

> Here's a govment that calls itself a govment, and lets on to be a govment, and thinks it is a govment, and yet's got to set stock-still for six whole months before it can take ahold of a prowling, thieving, infernal, white-shirted *free slave*. [Emphasis added][8]

You may ask what a "free slave" is, but that's simple. It's like a "married bachelor." Kowtowing to the culture, though cowardly perhaps, is always worse than kowtowing to logical consistency. Even more fun, at the end of the novel, when Miss Watson has already freed Jim in her will, the history-denying version of the novel reads, "Tom Sawyer had gone and took all that trouble and bother to set a free slave free!"

While Gribben, possibly unwittingly, doubles the irony of Twain's "set a free nigger free," the good professor denies history in another way. Jim is not the only slave to have ever been manumitted. Gribben apparently has made the decision it's worse to be falsely branded a "nigger" than a slave. The novel was set in 1840. Taking a look at the 1850 census report reveals that there were 424,390 "freed colored" in the nation, 122,703 in the South if we do not include Kentucky and Missouri as Southern states. Thus Gribben, by selecting "slave" rather than "colored" as his euphemism, denied freedom to 424,390 human beings rather than burden them with "the most inflammatory word in the English language."

History be damned in the name of political correctness.

But Gribben's justification for his expurgation is much like Bowdler's. "He hopes to introduce this book to a wider readership." Gribben wanted Twain to be available to people as sensitive and inferior as the politically correct. Bowdler wanted Shakespeare to be available to people as inferior as women. I would like to make both Shakespeare and Twain available to a wider readership. I mean, why exclude illiterates?

Nothing is more demeaning or embarrassing than not being able to sound out a word. To protect such sensitivities, we turn to Edward Dolch. In 1936, Dolch came up with a list of 220 words and a separate list of 95 nouns that comprise 50 to 75 percent of the words that children will encounter in school texts. So why not compile a Dolch-word Shakespeare? A great idea, huh? Dumbing down the verse would put the Bard within reach of an even wider readership than provided by Bowdler. To protect would-be readers from embarrassment, we will use the euphemism "Big Word" to substitute for any word not on Dolch's list. (I apologize that the word *word* is not on Dolch's list.)

Please join me as we consider the Dolch-word version of one of Hamlet's soliloquies, the most famous in the English language:

To be, or not to be—that is the (Big Word):
Big Word Big Word Big Word in the Big Word to Big
　Word
The Big Word and Big Word of Big Word Big Word
Or to take Big Word Big Word a see* of Big Word (*sea)
And by Big Word Big Word them....

I was, of course, like Bowdler and Gribben, careful not to add anything to the verse, but only to euphemize the phonetically offending words. My only motivation has been to introduce Shakespeare to a larger readership. And the same thing applies to Twain. Instead of offending readers with the hateful "free nigger" or confusing them with the illogical "free slave," I would modestly suggest "Big Word Big Word." This will place both Shakespeare and Twain within reach of those otherwise ill-equipped to enjoy them. I am merely striving for as much equality as possible in making the claim, "I am a better person and better equipped to understand the world because I have read and appreciated (euphemistically speaking) Shakespeare and Twain."

Equality rocks! Who can doubt it?

CHAPTER 14

SEXISM AND THE GREEKS

Everyone who knows anything of history also knows that great social revolutions are impossible without the feminine ferment. Social progress may be measured precisely by the social position of the fair sex (plain ones included).

—Karl Marx

L et's begin where we shouldn't. As a general rule, sex education is more fun when confined to the playground. There are exceptions. In my experience, sex education in the classroom has, upon occasion, had its merits. In 1959, for instance, Tom, Eddie, Barbara, and I, all seven- or eight-year-olds in second grade, failed to finish our seatwork. As punishment, we were left in the classroom while the other children got to go outside for recess.

I learned my lesson but possibly not one matching the teacher's lesson plan. Tom—who as a child in today's world of ADHD would have been medicated until he could no longer breathe—did a little finagling, a little coaching. Even though I cautiously stood behind the other boys, I can still remember my first peek. In case you've never taken one, men and women are different, about as equal in at least some qualities as apples and oranges. If you have any doubts, try eating both an orange and apple without peeling them.

Yes, men and women are just different. According to twentieth century journalist and professional cynic H. L. Menken, "Men have a much better time of it than women. For one thing, they marry later, for another, they die earlier."

If the sexes were equal, neither women nor diamonds would be treated as sex objects; pretty smiles and mansions would open neither doors nor hearts; fame and power might continue to seduce, but sex would lose its power. Neither feminists nor coquettes would throw men curves. The shapes of neither brain cells nor breasts would need to be banned from the battle between the sexes. There would be no maternity wards or paternity suits. In the Olympics, there would be just games, no men's and women's competitions; all would hurl the same discus, jump the same hurdles, or straddle roll the same balance beam—or not. During war, the battle deaths (and lusts) of men and women would be identical. Since life without choice is intolerable and choice without life is impossible, both fathers and mothers would know when life began; both would freely choose or reject the act to begin it.

However dicey generalities about the sexes may be, a few come to mind. To indulge in connubial bliss, men must learn to raise and lower the toilet seat; and while men train dogs to bite, women train dogs to beg. Couples tend to carry their canine training habits into marriage. Whether the union revolves around biting or begging depends on the favored trainer.

In our household, for instance, I am the undisputed lord and master. My first act was to place my wife in charge of everything. Thus, as any happily married man can appreciate, I reign supreme, doing exactly as I am commanded. Cliché being the popular vote on truth, allow me to borrow one known to most happily married men: "If mamma ain't happy, then no one is happy."

Not only are men and women different, for most of us that inequality is the motive force making the world go round. A world with equality of the sexes would work about as well as a battery with equality of the poles. As any parent of a teenage boy knows, God created Eve so that Adam would learn to brush his teeth and bathe. When it comes to sex, you reap what you sow; as a young man, I opened the door for the pretty girls; now they open it for me.

As I stressed in the introduction, I marry only women. You may, therefore, take this chapter with a grain of testosterone— which, I fear, is about all I have left. I am, in truth, a sexist. In my aged thinking, feminism revolves around politics, not truth. What truth is there in the belief that because the average woman was indoctrinated by men on what to believe, that the average woman should be indoctrinated on what to believe by women who, falling off the sexual bell curve, often have less in common with the thinking of the average woman than any well-trained husband does?

Not unlike many a feminist, I am more interested in cultivating the affections and loyalty of women than of men. Feminists have their reasons. So do I. You see, I specialize in treating problems with the use of the eyes that affect reading, learning, understanding, and sometimes attention. Softly falling through my mind, the impressions of forty years in my profession resemble a Renoir canvas dabbed with the delicately blended colors of women and children. Women are typically the driving force behind a child being brought to my office. If a woman has her husband's love and respect, a child gets care.

Should a woman be recognized for her strengths the same way a man is recognized for his strengths? Absolutely. I know, for instance, a brain scientist happily married to an astronaut. Despite their unique talents and pursuit of nontraditional roles, together they have raised a lovely family. If this is feminism, I'm all for it. However, if by feminism we mean hatred of, or having no use for, either one or the other sex or belittling women who play traditional roles in families, I hardly agree.

In the world of PC, prohibitions against sex have been replaced by prohibitions against sexism. But what exactly is sexism? Practically speaking, the term *sexism* is little more than an insipid insult hurled by the PC crew to discredit political opponents. In 2016, however, the Oxy Morons provided a workable definition: "prejudice, stereotyping, or discrimination, typically against women, on the basis of sex."

Following the lead of the morons, we can divide sexism into the "typical" and "atypical" varieties. Prejudice, stereotyping, or discrimination against women is "typical sexism." Prejudice, stereotyping, or discrimination against men (or women, perhaps, who choose traditional paths) is "atypical sexism." Using this division of sexism, many masculinists qualify as typical sexists; many feminists qualify as atypical sexists. PC prohibits typical sexism while applauding the more popular atypical variety. In this chapter, in an effort to maintain equality of the sexisms if not the sexes, we will assign the typical and atypical varieties equal sexism status.

GREEK SEXISM

Thank God for the Greeks. *Racism, sexism, Republicanism*—there would be no *isms* without the Greeks. Nothing lends credibility quite like Greek. Once the fractures of our hearts and minds were blamed on the whims of Greek gods; today we blame such fractures on the whims of Greek diagnoses. Greek miraculously turns poopy handwriting, poopy reading, and poopy arithmetic into *dysgraphia, dyslexia*, and *dyscalculia*—all pseudoscientific terms calculated to win educational accommodations, those handicaps necessary for winning the race to future earning potential despite a lack of academic talents. As anyone nurtured in PC understands, Greek provides more than an excuse for nonperformance. The classical language also provides the key to victimhood. *Xenophobia* and *homophobia* are Greek-based terms used to pass off as intelligent the moronic[1] speakers and writers using the terms.

To lend the term *sexist* weight and credence, it is often reinforced with the term *misogynist* from the Greek *miso* for a person who hates and *gynaeco* for woman or female. *Misogynist* was adopted into the English language in 1620 and held its own for almost four hundred years, the Oxy Morons in 1971 still defining *misogynists* as "women-haters." The last four decades have been much harder on the term. In 2016, the Morons updated the term to include "A person who hates, dislikes, or is prejudiced against woman."

Consider the use of *misogynist* in a sentence from 1878 by Thackeray: "'Confound all women, I say', muttered the young misogynist." In 1971, we would have known that Thackery was referring to a woman-hater. Now, we must muddle through. Was Thackery referring to misogyny or misogyny lite? Was

Thackery's character hateful of women or merely prejudiced against woman, dating only men perhaps?

The four-dollar Greek word for an atypical sexist is *misandrist*, again from *miso* for a person who hates and *andro* for man. The Oxy Morons tell us that the word entered the English language in my home town, Long Beach, California, appearing in the *Press-Telegram* in1952: "There is another more specific word, misandrist, which means a hater of male human beings." Interestingly, 1952 was the year of my birth. As a paperboy I once delivered the *Press-Telegram*. Go figure. Speakers of English have hated women for just shy of four-hundred years, but it took my birth to usher in hatred of men. Coincidence? Did three feminists follow my star?

Before 1952, we used *misanthrope* as "a hater of mankind: a man-hater; one who distrusts men and avoids their society." Back then, the feminists had yet to secede from mankind, so misanthropes hated the entire human race, not just the male half of it. It is encouraging to know that those ancient Greeks have opened their minds over the past century, allowing us to achieve equality of Greek pejoratives. Such usage happily allows typical and atypical sexists alike to exploit Greek for turning gender prejudices into a science. *Misogynists* now include those who are prejudiced against women dying on the battlefield, and *misandrists* include those who hate Y chromosomes. It is gratifying to see rhetoric keeping up with sexual politics. Having explored the role of Greek etiologies in the establishment of sexism, we now turn to the role of Greek goddesses.

WONDER WOMAN

Star-turned-superstar Gal Gadot[2]was the 2004 Miss Israel. She next served as a soldier and combat trainer in the

Israel Defense Forces. As soldier and beauty queen, she may be forgiven by even feminists. There is no chance of holding this woman, despite her being a mother, to the middle of the belle curve.

In 2017, Gadot was typecast as a Greek goddess in the title role of *Wonder Woman*, or so I believed the first time I saw the movie. Upon repeated viewings, however, I found that Gadot's beauty depends on more than her obvious inner and outer radiance magnified by her acting skills. Her transcendence as Diana Prince in *Wonder Woman* owes not just to nature, but to being nurtured by director Patty Jenkins, who rose above both typical and atypical sexism to craft the 700-million-dollars-plus-grossing *Wonder Woman* blockbuster into one of the most successful superhero movies in box office history—with no need for the demeaning "directed by a woman" to be added as it was at the time of the movie's opening weekend success.

Gadot is not new to being sized to fit roles. In the Tom Cruise and Cameron Diaz action/comedy movie *Knight and Day* (2010), Gadot plays Naomi, a sexy henchman for a crime boss. The director, James Mangold (*Walk the Line*), sizes down the five-foot-ten Gadot to not tower over the five-foot-seven Cruise. Similarly, in *Batman versus Superman*, director Zach Snider (*Man of Steel*, *Suicide Squad*) transforms a sexy Gal into nothing more than a sexy superhero—sexy enough, however, to make *Super Woman* the most anticipated superhero film of the next season.

When Patty Jenkins is given her chance, however, she creates not just another sexy superhero but a Greek goddess. In every still scene, using camera angle, costume, makeup, and only God knows what kind of digital enhancing, Jenkins lovingly sculpts Diana Prince's beauty into the stuff of art, not sex. Diana seemingly walks apart, largely because as the camera cuts between Diana and others, Jenkins takes every opportunity to frame the heroine to fill more of the screen, subtly reinforcing her godhood. The other characters, both men and women, are astonished by Diana's beauty and seem like children in her presence.

The story begins on Themyscira, a hidden island refuge from mankind, peopled with Amazon warriors obsessively training for battle lest their female paradise be disturbed by the unfair sex. Diana is raised to believe that Zeus created his beloved mankind and that his jealous son Ares, the god of war, poisoned men's minds with a compulsion for conflict. Zeus created the Amazons to save mankind from themselves. In truth Zeus, using Hippolyta for the purpose, fathered Diana that she might kill Ares. Unaware that she is a demigoddess, Diana is raised to believe that her mother sculpted her from clay and that Zeus brought her to life.

As British spy Steve Trevor (played by Chris Pine) crashes his plane on Themyscira, Diana is still a complete innocent. Her wonder at viewing a world transcending her habitual actions makes her, and us, conscious. For the audience, the experience is like exploring Disney World in a fresh way through the eyes of a child. When Diana, for instance, finds Steve standing naked before her, having just bathed in a rejuvenating pool, she examines him with a clinical eye and asks if he is a "typical" example of his sex. When he modestly confesses to being "above average," she asks him, "What is that?" He stammers until he discovers she has changed the subject to his watch. He tries to explain what time is and how the watch tells him when to eat and sleep. Her reply, "You let this little thing tell you what to do?" We hope she is referring to the timepiece.

That Diana views the male-dominated world with the same wonder and skepticism that she viewed the watch allows feminists to claim the movie as their own. On the Internet, we find such articles as Andrew Dyce's "Wonder Woman: 15 Movie Moments that Crush Sexism" and Zoe Williams's "Why Wonder Woman Is a Masterpiece of Subversive Feminism." In truth, the movie captures not only typical sexism/misogyny, as these article titles suggest, but atypical sexism/misandry as well. The typical sexism is well covered in the above articles, leaving me to highlight a sampling of the misandrous examples.

Themyscira is an island paradise. It has no men. Diana is schooled that men are essential for "procreation, but unessential for pleasure." When the armed Hippolyta first sees Steve standing next to her daughter, she immediately imagines the worst and commands him, "Step away from her." When Hippolyta gets closer to Steve, she lunges as if to dispatch him but is stopped by Diana with the words, "No, Mother!" Another Amazon nevertheless judges, "We should kill him now!" Hippolyta warns her daughter, "Men are easily corrupted," and "Be careful in the world of men—they do not deserve you!" The Amazon Queen, though trying to protect her daughter from stereotypically imagined men, might qualify as an atypical sexist, a "man-hater" or, in our lexicon, a "misandrist." If she hates men, it is not because of Amazon strength, it is because she is terrified that her daughter is no match for the male Ares.

Being a demigod, not a woman, Diana takes no side in the battle between the sexes. Her goodness and bravery transcends both forms of sexism. She is not there to protect "women's rights." She sees herself as part of "the bridge for a greater understanding of all men." She believes, "If no one else will defend the world from Ares, I must." When Hippolyta suggests that World War I is mankind's problem, Diana takes ownership of the conflict, exclaiming, "It's not *their* war." She later explains to her mother the reason she must leave the safety of the island, find Ares, and stop World War I: "I cannot stand by while innocent lives are lost!" And "I'm willing to fight for those who cannot fight for themselves." Diana knows that as an Amazon, it is her "sacred duty to defend the world."

It is not until the end of the movie that Diana finally confronts Ares, finds that her father is Zeus, and learns that she is a goddess. Her brother, Ares, comes near to defeating her by channeling her power into rage against men. It is only when she recalls her love for Steve, a mortal male who sacrificed himself that others might live, that the full power of her godhead is revealed to her—and us.

Andrew Dyce, in his crush-sexism article, writes: "Diana knows that every human being is deserving of the same respect." But as Diana assure us, "It's not about deserve; it's about what you believe"—this after Ares has reminded us that men are "cruel, selfish," "evil," "capable of the greatest horrors," "ugly, filled with hatred, weak," causing "pain, suffering, and destruction." He sounds like a lobbyist for a feminist political action committee. Diana sees "the darkness that ends with man's light" and agrees with Ares that men are all these things, but "so much more."

Where a male director would have created a sexy battle epic, Patty Jenkins, from her female viewpoint, has captured transcendence. When the war ends, not only do soldiers kiss

LAUGHING AT POLITICAL CORRECTNESS

their sweethearts, but fathers hold their children. Jenkins transforms a talented, stunningly beautiful actress into a selfless, heroic goddess, not just another superhero.

Jenkin's triumph in directing this movie is a lesson for typical and atypical sexists, misogynists and misandrists alike—a lesson for all of us. As a female in Hollywood she has probably seldom gotten what she deserved. In *Wonder Woman,* however, she has gotten what she believes as she proves that sometimes women are not equal, they are better, and it is better to win in the Hollywood competition than to waste time belittling men and crying about the unfairness of their privileges.

We owe *isms* and *ists* to the Greeks. *Sexism* is a term used as a weapon in the battle between the sexes, a term to divide rather than unite the sexes. *Sexist* is a term to dehumanize one being while trapping another in the go-nowhere status of a victim. Feminists place themselves at risk when recruiting Diana as their poster child. The movie *Wonder Woman* is hardly about women's rights. It is about human rights, raising both women and men to greater heights.

The movie captures the battle raging inside of all of us to choose good or evil, self or selflessness. The measurement of Jenkin's art is not in her sex, but how that art inspires us to find the humaneness too often shrouded by our humanity. We realize we are less than we could be, but so much more than we sometimes appear. The movie raises our consciousness as only art, not sexual politics, can—a lesson for both typical and atypical sexists, misogynists and misandrists. We can thank Zeus for *Wonder Woman* and the Greeks.

CHAPTER 15

THE HATE SPEECH OF POLITICAL CORRECTNESS

I have never hated a man enough to give him his
diamonds back.

—*Zsa Zsa Gabor*

Hatred is a subject near and dear to all of us. Where would
we be without it? I especially love hating the hypocrisy of
those who hate people who hate people, those who fight
hate speech with even more heartfelt hate speech of their own.
These haters of hate threaten the very fabric of our society:
the freedom of speech needed to understand and resolve
differences. Which is worse, a racist using skin-think to justify
changing or preserving the social status quo, or the NMM
threatening reputations or livelihoods for violations of PC?

WILL THE REAL HATE SPEECH STAND UP?

Like most of the vocabulary of PC, the definition of *hate
speech* defies logic. How can conservative bias qualify as hate
speech while liberal bias qualifies as love? Reconsider the
earlier-visited love speech of Madonna: "Yes, I'm angry. Yes,

I'm outraged. Yes, I have thought an awful lot about blowing up the White House." While only freedom of speech stands between Madonna and jail, imagine the cries of "hate speech" if President Obama still resided at 1600 Pennsylvania Ave and, say, Mel Gibson were the protestor yearning to dynamite the White House. Like *racism* and *xenophobia*, *hate speech* is a false category, capturing no essence of nature. A real category like *gold* remains gold viewed from any perspective; the false category *hate speech* owes its essence more to perspective than nature. To define *hate speech*, look no further than the biases of the speaker doing the hating.

In truth, hate *is* in the eyes of the beholder. Only fools imagine that the hater provides anything but a caricature of the object of hatred. Just as all books reveal the author, his research, biases, and ability to hide or not hide behind words, so all speech reveals the speaker, but not necessarily the subject addressed.

For years we spoke of Pluto as a planet. This was about us and our addiction to scientific groupthink, not Pluto. Similarly, my hatred of spring springs from my allergies, not any particular offense of spring itself. My hatred is about me, not spring. Spring has earned my hatred no more than President Trump has earned the hatred of progressives. We are all protesting our own limitations of thought, vision, or, perhaps, power.

To those with the slightest qualifications as skeptics, hate speech is about the heart of the hater, not the hated. At its best, or worst, hate speech is a flimsy excuse for making bad choices—violence being one such bad choice. But as we have said, anything, even the Golden Rule, can provide an excuse for bad choices: if I treat myself with hate, the Golden Rule is my license to hate everyone else as well. If we are looking for an excuse to kick freedom of speech out of our Constitution, why shake a finger at hate speech? Why not abolish the Golden Rule?

What qualifies as hate speech is to be found in the *particularity* of the hater or hated. The Oxy Morons, for instance, define hate speech as "(a) a speech or address inciting hatred or intolerance, esp. towards a particular social group on the basis of ethnicity, religious beliefs, sexuality, etc.; (b) . . . speech (or sometimes written material) inciting such hatred or intolerance."

When we were laughing at political correctness in Chapter 3, we discussed the elusive term *particular* and how it is used to squeeze universal terms to fit politics. No one, for instance, defines *love* as affinity for *particular* groups. The universal isn't tailored. The term *hate speech*, however, with pretenses of being some sort of universal, is little more than politics masquerading as morality.

Who is *particular* enough to qualify as a recipient of "hate speech"? If spoken or written materials generate hate or intolerance against racists, sexists, nativists, homophobes, xenophobes, or speakers of hate, this hardly qualifies as hate speech because the deplorable and proud are not *particular* enough to deserve protection from abusive language. If we publicly proclaim that Jesus Christ is Lord, is this hate speech because the proclamation might create intolerance against Muslims who equate Jesus with a prophet, not God? Do declarations of God's death fail to qualify as hate speech, because Christian beliefs are not *particular* enough to be protected? As we noted in chapter 3, political correctness is the hate speech voted most likely to succeed. Hate speech, it turns out, is merely the rhetoric of a particular political party—the wrong one, obviously.

THE ULTIMATE HATE SPEECH

The ultimate hate speech is not to be found in such hollow terms as *racism, sexism, nativism, homophobia, xenophobia, intolerance,* or even *hate speech*. The ultimate hate speech is to be found in two words: "Shut up!" If the eyes are the windows to the soul, the mouth is the door. Our words define us, reveal us, control our minds. To say, "Shut up" is to say, "I have no interest in you, your beliefs, feelings, fears, aspirations, prejudices, foolishness, or wisdom. Succumb to the control of my own."

"Shut up" is hate speech preparing to tumble into violence. Race, sex, country, religion, sexual perversion—hatred of any one of these falls short of hatred of the person. A self is not his sex, race, country, religion, or perversions. To so reduce a person belittles him. A command to silence does more than belittle; it attempts to abolish the entire human being.

To abridge freedom of speech is like abridging a book; to command silence is like burning one. While the listener has every right to refuse to listen, he has no right to command others not to listen. Such a command is hate speech at its worst, a command to abolish freedom of speech.

THE CONTAGION OF HATE

Hate reduces the hater, not the hated. Jesus recommended, "Whosoever shall smite thee on thy right cheek, turn to him the other also.... Love your enemies.... Do good to them that hate you." The philosophy of the sermon has withstood the test of time. Take a moment to think of someone who has treated you or your loved ones like dirt, someone who has "deserved" your hatred. Or—if you love your enemies but have hated this book—think about me.

Good. Feel better? Did thinking about a person who has earned your hate turn you into a kinder, happier person? Do slurs such as *racist, sexist,* or *homophobe*[1] really flow from the milk of human kindness, or are they but examples of the most vicious hate speech to crowd today's popular press? Pity the politically correct. They must feel terrible with all their pent-up hate for the deplorable and proud.

The only inoculation to hate is to learn to turn the other cheek, to pray for those who persecute us, to strengthen our tools of debate by dissecting the arguments of our opponents rather than dissecting the idiots who argue against us.[2] The reason we hate those who abuse us is that we become just like them. Our response reveals the worst in us, to others and ourselves, as we descend to the level of our abusers. We become haters ourselves, no better than the haters we hate. If instead we turn the other cheek, then we only have to live with their hatred, not our own. And in the long, long, long run, our own hatred is the only hatred with consequences. And if, perhaps, readers care to contradict me, I hate them all.

FIGHT HATE VS. FLIGHT HATE

But what is hate? The word *hate* hearkens back to those smoldering Vikings and Germans. We could reasonably divide *hate* into two varieties, the first suggesting intense animosity, loathing, and a pinch of malice; the second suggesting distaste or dislike. If we think about the two terms, the first hate inspires destruction; the second, avoidance. To use a scientific metaphor, the first hate inspires "fight"; the second, "flight."

Hating gamblers and prostitutes would cause flight haters to avoid Las Vegas and fight haters to hold demonstrations and public-relations smear campaigns against Las Vegas. Similarly, "white flight" would qualify as flight hate; trying to destroy the reputations of the whites who flew would qualify as fight hate. When asked to marry, the flight hater would simply say no, the fight hater would as soon see the proposer beheaded.

Fight hate and flight hate are, to my thinking, two different animals. Personally, I would rather be fled than attacked. To the politically correct, however, just as racism is racism so hate is hate, and jokesters and fleers deserve to be hated with full fight hate, their reputations shattered by the hater's animosity, loathing, and malice.

Hate speech is largely ubiquitous. Chiropractors and orthopedic surgeons are guilty of hate speech—if many could, they would put each other out of business. Tax lawyers and tax accountants are guilty of hate speech. Oral surgeons and plastic surgeons are guilty of hate speech. Optometrists and medical supremacists are guilty of hate speech. Protestants and Catholics are guilty of hate speech. Progressives and conservatives are guilty of hate speech. The politically correct and incorrect are guilty of hate speech. The basket of pseudo-saints and the basket of deplorables are guilty of hate speech. You and I are guilty of hate speech. The only way to end hate speech is for everyone to just shut up!

RISING ABOVE HATE SPEECH

The real problem with hate speech is not the hate, it's the distraction. The very concept of hate speech distracts us from getting from point A to point B. Focusing our attention on hate speech focuses our attention on our victimhood, not our goals—unless our goal, and only claim to fame, is to be a victim. It turns us into tattletales rather than into those getting the job done. It ties our hands to the past rather than freeing them to reach for the future. And if we define injustice as anytime we lost the game being played, whether football, baseball, war, politics, economics, social status—take your pick—then there is a whole lot of injustice going on, a whole lot of victimhood, a whole lot of distraction from getting on with the game.

Let's imagine hate speech in action. Hank Aaron hit 755 homeruns. Suppose that Hank had been more concerned with hate speech than winning. Suppose that when he was at bat in the 1950s a racist in the stands had used the n-word to distract him from his batting—not that anyone in the 1950s would have used the n-word and not that anyone would have wasted time being distracted by it. Now if Hank had been trained in political correctness and sensitized to the consummate evils of hate speech, he could have thrown his bat down and gone over to the umpire and, in tears, have complained that some mean and nasty man had called him the n-word, and said his parents weren't married, and questioned his intimacy with his mother, and all sorts of hateful things. He could have said he was too upset to go on playing until someone punished the nasty man who had offended him. Or he could have ignored the pitiful spectator and knocked another ball into the stands—just for spite. As it turns out, blaming our failures on the hate speech of others is an excuse for, not a solution to, our problems. What others say does not justify our own neglect of taking responsibility for our lives.

Perhaps instead of wasting our time worrying about hate speech, we should listen to the Roman emperor and philosopher Marcus Aurelius who philosophized, "It's silly to try to escape other people's faults. They are inescapable. Just try to escape your own." He also wrote about the "tranquility that comes when you stop caring what they say. Or think, or do. Only what you do. (Is this fair? Is this the right thing to do?)." Instead Aurelius advised us "not to be distracted by their darkness. To run straight for the finish line, unswerving." Sure, Marcus Aurelius spoke almost two thousand years before we got enlightenment and the glorious indignity and distraction of hate speech, but even the politically correct should feel safe in believing him—he persecuted Christians, so he couldn't have been all bad, now could he?

Those who are out to win on their merits and choices rather than their cruel fate and victimhood just don't have time to worry about remarks that are made for no other reason than to distract them from success. It is the thickness, not the color, of our skin that matters. It is keeping our eyes on the ball, not listening to halfwits baiting us from the stands. That's why spectators are spectators rather than players; if they knew how to hit homeruns, they wouldn't waste their time on hate speech. It was taking the right pitches rather than taking offense that allowed Hank Aaron to break the Babe's homerun record—despite the dismay of those weighed down by their own skin-think.

In our first chapter, I mentioned that I was an optometrist and that medical supremacists had done everything they could to crush my profession. When I began, optometrists were not allowed to lease space in medical buildings. We were not allowed to author papers in medical journals. We were not allowed to attend medical academy meetings. Every five or ten years, the same supremacists distributed the same tired position statement to educators cautioning them that vision was not related to reading and that correcting eye-muscle coordination problems would not improve the ability to learn. The supremacists constantly assured the public that we lacked the blind studies needed to prove what we do. When the National Eye Institute funded the demanded blind studies, Mayo Clinic, Bascom Palmer, and seven optometry schools joined forces to show that the exercises reduced headaches, loss of place, and loss of concentration when reading. In their next position statement, the supremacists presented a single practitioner's cases to refute the conclusion of the gold standard National Eye Institute study.

Today, our group is still neither liked nor respected by the medical supremacists, but it hardly matters. More and more, their continued petty attacks cost them far more in respect from the allied professions than it gained them. Despite the supremacists keeping our services barred from insurance reimbursement, we are flourishing and prospering as never before.

Sure, when we get together, we enjoy commiserating with one another about the unfairness of one profession dominating all of healthcare, but it's not our feeling sorry for ourselves that has brought us success. It's our dedication to helping patients and those patients posting on the Internet their successes (while that Internet has not been shut down in homage to hate speech) that has allowed us to bypass the medical monopoly—not to mention that respect for medicine has dwindled as both patient and physician values have been replaced with a love-hate relationship with insurance companies.

It's like we covered in the chapter on toleration, success in sales is not about being thought right. It's not about being complimented or praised. It's not about the customers treating us with respect. It's not about taking offense. It's about making the sale, not wasting attention on being the victim of hate speech. Make the sale and deliver more than promised. Those who would stick our attention on hate speech are not our friends. They deny we have free will and that our choices in life maximize or minimize our providence, no matter if in the overall scheme of this world our share of providence is big or small.

SUMMARY

Reviewing our chapters on PC run amok, the politically correct have tossed us into the basket of deplorables; created the hate speech to end all hate speech; dehumanized us as *ists* and *phobes*; fashioned verbal handicaps to balance the race between races; chased the rainbow of the equality delusion even if it meant reducing the able into idiots; limited language to achieve what limited ability could not; enforced our silence to drown out our process of thought; mimicked nature in placing the empty half of the glass on top; sought to control our minds by controlling our communication; created a mental vacuum through which free speech could not travel; fashioned a language game in which only the blind didn't have to play dumb; masqueraded politics as morality; denied us the right to say no to relationships; engineered a one-way road with the traffic flow determined by imagined rights instead of road signs; defined inhumanity according to the group; restricted our right to remain silent; judged injustice by the color of its skin; placed group rights over human rights; celebrated the diversity of heritage over the diversity of great ideas; allowed silent envy to warp perception into confusing property ownership with greed; promulgated freedom of boycott over freedom of speech; rewarded freedom of excuse over freedom of choice; threatened closing our doors if we open our mouths; acted as the pawns for the elitists who hope to own the game rather than play it; proved Aristotle correct by confusing the equality of votes with the equality of voters; imagined that controlling language could turn losers into winners; invented an algebra in which only one side of the equation was equal; denied freedom of speech, thus providing the next tyrant to come along with a turnkey dictatorship; robbed the able to support the equal; and created the intolerance to end all intolerances.

So what?

Get over it, and get on with the pursuit of happiness and free speech. If we are angry or outraged, who is to blame? Perhaps we should return to our Roman emperor friend Marcus Aurelius and his stoical advice:

> These things have no hold on the soul. They stand there unmoving, outside it. Disturbance comes only from within—from our own perceptions. Choose not to be harmed—and you won't feel harmed. Don't feel harmed—and you haven't been.... Nothing that goes on in anyone else's mind can harm you. Nor can the shifts and changes in the world around you. —Then where is harm to be found? In your capacity to see it. Stop doing that and everything will be fine.

The stoics essentially believed that we are responsible for the stories we allow into our minds. Genesis or Darwin, providence or the swirl of atoms, free will or free excuse, victimhood or reaping what we sow, human rights or group rights, eternity or oblivion—the world and its public relation experts will continue to spin until they stop, but the stories we allow into our heads need never end so long as consciousness and our imagined freedom of choice inspire us onward. No one but ourselves can disturb our peace. No matter the sound of hate speech striking eardrums; only we can sully the sand running through the eternity-glass of the soul.

My advice? Stay focused. Say no to the new terrorism, but never confuse free speech against hate with hate against free speech. If a business condemns the words it perceives to be hate speech, fine. This is free speech against hate, not hate against free speech. But if a business abridges free speech, proclaiming its allegiance to PC by publicly firing another celebrity, this is hate against free speech, not free speech against hate. It's time to protest and take our business elsewhere.

Despite the teachings of the New Moral Majority, loss of freedom of speech is a far, far greater evil than racism, sexism, nativism, homophobia, xenophobia, intolerance, and hate speech combined, for all of these will perish only if speech remains free. Don't swing at the hate speech of political correctness; keep your eyes on the ball of liberty.

CHAPTER 16

KEEPING UP APPEARANCES
—DIVERSITY AND TRUTH

Familiarity breeds contempt.... The reason we hold
truth in such respect is because we have so little
opportunity to get familiar with it.

—*Mark Twain*

There is a terrible irony to be found in diversity. Diversity has become the uniform rallying cry of PC. PC imagines that equality is equal to diversity and that, therefore, diversity is a goal to be cherished, espoused, and engineered. Not all diversities, however, are equal. Diversity is also the rallying cry of the white supremacists who fear that intermarriages such as mine, if pursued for enough generations, will end diversity with all heritages merging back into their African roots. Still, it is heartwarming to find the politically correct and the white supremacists can agree on the need for diversity even though one group wants diversity today, the other group, diversity tomorrow.

Imagine a dream of a politically correct party containing the fair skin of Scandinavian blonds and Irish redheads and the olive skin of raven-haired gypsies; the clean-shaven faces of accountants and bearded chins of explorers; the wearers of turbans, yarmulkes, burqas, and habits; the darkness of Africans and Australian aborigines and the skin-tone spectrum of Asian Indians and African Americans; and the close, horizontal eyelids of the Chinese and the beautiful almond-shaped eyes of women such as my Vietnamese wife. Imagine seeing women wearing trousers and closely cropped hair and men with flowing locks and flowing skirts, the outlines of their bras visible beneath the cover of their blouses, and seeing tall, anorexic models as well as voluptuous figures overflowing the edges of measurement, and seeing the scale and body builders flexing and the profoundly cerebral palsied trembling and drooling in their wheelchairs. And most importantly imagine that this spectrum of this diversity *all* hate President Trump.

Ah, yes. Diversity! A surfeit of exotic appearances with a uniformity in narrowness of mind.

One of the many possible definitions of *racism*, we could imagine, is the confusing of appearance with ideas, confusing the cover of a book with its contents. PC has diminished diversity to the same level of superficiality, reducing variation to appearances. Like racism, diversity has become playing the odds that appearance can predict intellect, politics, ability, ideologies, or competence. In the dream party scene above, the politically correct would make the assumption that the room was full of liberals rather than those with the intelligence and sense of humor needed to step back and joke and laugh at each other's incongruities and peculiarities.

And, oh yes—what if I lied about the Trump thing? What if I failed to mention that the described dream party was a celebration of Trump's victory over the scientific probability of the *New York Times*? Unlikely? Impossible? That's what we get when we are guilty of prejudging people and their beliefs according to the mix of their appearances.

In the land of equality and PC, some diversities, it turns out, are more equal and correct than others. The pantheon of diversity condemns intolerance of off-color skin but commands intolerance of off-color jokes. Diversity embraces those disadvantaged by gluttony, envy, or sloth, but not those disadvantaged by greed or—heaven forbid—Christianity.

I believe in a less homogeneous, more diverse appreciation of diversity. The value of diversity in appearance belongs more to the study of decoration and aesthetics than ideas. The real value of diversity is not in appearance, but thought. Diversity of thought and great ideas is not so much a prize to be sought as a vehicle for being conveyed, however slowly, along the road to truth.

TRUTH EMERGING

What is truth? Would we, any more than Pontius Pilate, recognize Truth if we were looking it in the eyes as He stood before us?

Somehow truth revolves around the relationship between actions and stories, but philosophers are divided in their thoughts on the exact nature of this relationship. Imagine a puzzle picturing the Resurrection. If truth is absolute, the puzzle picture is true because the Resurrection is absolutely true—not to beg the question. If truth is relative, the puzzle's truth rests on its solvers. If truth is the correspondence between action and story, then the picture is true because it exactly corresponds to the exact physical actions and appearances of the Resurrection. If truth depends on the coherence of the story, the puzzle is true if the pieces all fit together. If truth rests on good old American pragmatism, then the puzzle is true if it is good for us to assemble it.

My own favorite story on truth we could call "the emergence theory of truth." In this story, truth emerges[1] from the sum of the possible viewpoints of the puzzle. Although only God has access to all viewpoints, including our own, the more viewpoints we consider, the closer we may (or may not) creep toward truth.

In the nineteenth century, John Stuart Mill put it this way: "The only way in which a human being can make some approach to knowing the whole of a subject is by hearing what can be said about it by persons of every variety of opinion, and studying all modes in which it can be looked at by every character of the mind."[2]

Similarly, the nineteenth-century poet Walt Whitman wrote, "You shall listen to all sides and filter them from your self."[3]

In the twentieth century, philosopher of science Paul Feyerabend put it much the same way:

> Knowledge . . . is not a series of self-consistent theories that converges toward an ideal view. It is rather an ever increasing *ocean of mutually incompatible alternatives*, each single theory, each fairy-tale, each myth that is part of the collection forcing the others into greater articulation and all of them contributing, via this process of competition, to the development of our consciousness. Nothing is ever settled. No view can ever be omitted from a comprehensive account.[4]

It could be argued that to know God's Word is to know truth. But can we completely understand a speaker's words if we do not fully know the speaker's mind? When the father says, "Don't go outside," does the child really know what the father means by "outside"? The child's perception of what exists beyond the door may differ profoundly from the father's. The child knows what he needs to know not to go outdoors even though he has no concept of the truth of "outdoors." He knows his father's words, but not his father's mind; he does not know the truth of the dangers that the father perceives.

A verse is not a chapter; a chapter, a book; a book, The Book. Scripture brings us ever closer to the Truth we know by the name of God, but the apostle Paul knew, wrote, and lived the Scriptures and never imagined he knew the full truth: "When I was a child, I spake as a child, I understood as a child, I thought as a child: but when I became a man, I put away childish things. For now we see through a glass, darkly; but then face to face: now I know in part; but then shall I know even as also I am known."

Truth is more than words; it's actions. A perfect cake recipe is known truly to the baker of perfect cakes; a perfect bow and arrow, to the archer who never misses the mark; Scripture, which is perfect, to the soul without sin. If we compare our understanding of Scripture now to when we were younger, we may find our viewpoints have increased in number as our actions have expanded and understanding grown. Even older theologians, familiar with all written viewpoints, might, agreeing with Paul, await a fuller truth. In other words, truth cannot earn its whole-truth capital T until the last of the viewpoints known to God have been viewed.

To the skeptic, certain knowledge is difficult in the presence of ignorance. We may, for instance, know we are sitting on a sofa, but could still be lost. We might fail to know where the sofa is in the room, the room is in the building, the building is in the world, or the world is in the universe. As long as we remain ignorant of the full construction of our universe and any others that may exist behind the limits of our finite minds, to claim a certain knowledge of truth is to replace ignorance with arrogance.

Certain faith is another matter. All but hypocrites admit their debt to faith: faith in God, science, philosophy, groupthink, experience, reason, probability, intelligence, stupidity, and/or passion. For all the skeptic knows with absolute certainty, we could be dreaming, but we still must have the faith to go on using the restroom. Those who deny such faith have to pee really bad.

FLEETING FACTS

The obvious objection to the emergence theory of truth is suspicion about being perverted by false viewpoints. How can untruth lead to truth? Stories about eating babies, for instance, cannot lead to truth. Right?

Maybe or maybe not. Take, for instance, Jonathan Swift, the Irish satirist and author of *Gulliver's Travels*. In 1729, probably suffering from hunger pangs cause by a diet, Swift wrote a scrumptious essay, "A modest proposal for preventing the children of poor people from being a burthen to their parents or the country, and for making them beneficial to the public."[5]

Swift's ingenious solution to Irish poverty and starvation was to—instead of aborting and murdering Irish children—

eat them. As Swift wrote, "I have been assured by a very knowing American of my acquaintance in London, that a young healthy child, well nursed, is at a year old a most delicious, nourishing, and wholesome food, whether *stewed, roasted, baked,* or *boiled."* Swift reinforced his waste-not-want-not philosophy by suggesting the skinning of the infants to "make admirable *gloves for ladies,* and *summer boots for fine gentlemen."* Swift's words, though entirely false, threw into relief the shabby treatment of the Irish poor by the self-righteous English. His 1729 essay is still famous, and continues to highlight the value of even a bad idea in contributing to the search for truth. Such can be the fruit of thinking outside the box—or inside the basket.

The search is not over until all possible viewpoints have been explored. We are not interested in diversity so much as completeness. In this view, all news can be regarded as fake news until all the viewpoints have been reported; it doesn't matter if the reported parts of the story cohere or agree with both each other and today's groupthink. It doesn't matter if the reported parts of the story precisely correspond to past actions.

The truth, for instance, of the Civil War is not to be found in only the maps and the memoirs of generals and the dusty volumes of historians. The truth is also to be found in the stories of slaves and politicians; the Federalist's twenty-four-decade passion for increasing central power versus the Antifederalist's twenty-four-decade passion for maintaining local power; the stories of technologies that, without killing 600,000 people, might have eventually replaced slavery; the stories of crushed family lines; the stories found in the letters of soldiers to their sweethearts, the stories scribbled in the diaries of mothers who lost fathers, husbands, or sons. Until all the viewpoints have been reported, all the stories told, we may still fall short of the truth of the Civil War.

Sure, there are facts, but we confuse them with truth at our peril. Facts are fleeting, truth persists. As we have considered elsewhere, it was once a fact that there were nine planets, that the heavens were immutable, that the continents were anchored in place on the globe, that light was a wave, that space and time were absolute. Facts change. Truth is known to the Being with all viewpoints at His disposal. Only when we know what that Being knows will vengeance be ours. Until then, we will have to suck it up, put the past in the past, and get on with creating the future.

If truth emerges from the sum of the viewpoints, then the truth is not to be found in such philosophers as Plato, Aristotle, or Descartes. Rather we may inch closer to the truth by exploring all philosophy, theology, science, and personal experience—providing that all philosophy, theology, science, and experience won't, like a mystery or thriller, end with a plot twist. Only time and diversity of thought will tell, but not if diversity of thought is censored by PC. Outside of the potential for nuclear holocaust exploding the arrogance of scientific predictions about global warming, PC is our nation's greatest threat, for PC destroys free speech and blinds us to the diversity of thought that might throw a truer truth into relief.

CONCLUSIONS

In this book, we have tried to think outside the politically correct box. We have questioned definitions fabricated to destroy lives. We have pointed out inconsistencies. We haven't, however, discredited individuals instead of their arguments. We haven't told any empathetic tales calculated to tear out hearts for the purpose of winning arguments through emotion. Those tales we will save for those adept at bleeding-heart politics, for no tale, however empathetically heart-rending, tells us the best way to avoid rendering hearts in the future. The picture of a starving child or the atrocities of war does not tell us the best way to reduce misery and postpone for a little time suffering and death on planet Earth. We, therefore, welcome those diverse political tales that best bring into contrast our own. No tale should be left unturned in the search for truth—no matter what PC demands.

With this in mind, the next time you dream of a politically correct party, take along all the subgroups of Americans you can—Asian, African, and European. Just don't forget the deplorable and proud—the racist, nationalist, sexist, xenophobe, homophobe, intolerant speaker of hate, and maybe even a deplorable conservative or two. Do it in the name of diversity. And remember back to when this book began. In those first pages, I promised a polemic and noted that every story has two sides but a polemic has only one. I noted that it was not my job to buy the unbalanced arguments in these chapters, only to sell them. I even denied that the book reflected the opinion of the author and not to go boycotting me if anything is politically incorrect. So, don't.

One more question before we go. What turns stories into literature? In my imagination, at least, literature not only amuses, it invites us to open our eyes and explore ourselves, others, and the world. It allows us to embrace the same consciousness we experience at the sight of a sunset or the tremor of desire in a true love's eyes.

Nothing kills consciousness quite like habit, groupthink, cliché, routine, familiarity, or the politically correct party line—these breed unconsciousness. Cushioned by groupthink, we live habitual, automated, largely unconscious lives, sitting in the same easy chair, sleeping on the same side of the bed, eating with the same hand, driving the same way to work, and, with luck, kissing the same spouse (some of us being more disciplined than others).

In my work as a vision therapist changing the way patients see the world, I've found that vision is much the same way. We see what we expect to see. A chair is a chair; a table, a table. But if, like artists, we see the negative space cradling the table and chair, then the world beckons freshly, time opens anew. We abandon a stale world of words and prefabricated images to sculpt fresh worlds of experience and space. We explore the diversity of perception. We leave the habitual world behind and become conscious of the now, not the earlier or later. We learn, grow, and outstrip memory.

Just as novelty creates exploration and consciousness, so can questions. Therefore, let's summarize some questions already asked. Do we, for instance, dehumanize groups when we pretend they have no reason to blush? Have we traded the bullying of one political moral majority for another? Do we have a right to say no to relationships, to kisses and contracts? Does unabridged freedom of speech include the freedom to remain silent and freedom to hear even what others hate? Can morality be defined by grassroots politics irrigated by overflow from the wrong creek? If Beyoncé and I are equal in the voting booth, does that make us equal in the concert hall or ticket sales, as guaranteed by a government intent on proving our equality? Is equal treatment under the law the goal of a free republic? Are laws to make us equal more often delusions used to justify treating us unequally? When it comes to locking our doors at night and screening nannies and the holders of green cards, is xenophobia just another word for common sense? Is the oldest profession in the world great in America because our immigration laws keep out the competition—and should we have kept out lawyers instead? Is talk of human rights essential and talk of group rights politics? Is racism the use of skin-think to justify treating others as we would not like to be treated? Is racism the use of skin-think to justify maintaining or abandoning the status quo? Is it sexist not to treat men and women as equals—especially in athletic events? Do terms like *racism* and *sexism* really cut nature at the joints, or are they the products of groupthink dictating thought even as they spread the contagion of hate?

In these chapters, I have attempted to tell stories inviting us to explore PC, the New Moral Majority, and the basket of deplorables from a different perspective. If I have opened consciousness with a novel viewpoint or question, then I have done my job in adding to diversity of thought and maybe even the search for truth. If I have provided readers with words to describe the stories in their hearts, then I have done my job even better.

Still, there are yet stories undiscovered, unexplored, and untold to be discovered, explored, and told . . . but only if we dare to be deplorable and proud and to ignore PC long enough to discover, explore, and tell those stories. When we hear the word *diversity,* let us not descend to reducing humanity and politics to the coverings on heads, the shapes of eyes, the texture of hair, or the color of skin. Instead of equating diversity with something as shallow as appearance, let's applaud a diversity of great ideas—even if some of those ideas spark outrage in the popular elections of groupthink during this moment in capricious history.

I suggest we treat ideas with laughter even as we treat the person standing before us with dignity and kindness—rather than the treatment they probably deserve, the treatment we probably deserve. So long as the stream of ideas continues to flow, we will never stand in quite the same nation twice. Free speech is the price we pay for the upkeep of our Bill of Rights. We cannot let PC stop the payments.

Today PC is America's greatest threat, for no right of special interest groups is as precious to all of us, special interest groups included, as freedom of speech. We are our stories. To silence those stories is to deny and control our very souls. Take away freedom of speech, and when the republic falls from the wall of liberty there will be no King's English and no free mind to put that republic back together again. We cannot let PC abridge our free speech. Don't be afraid to remain deplorable and proud.

We owe it to our nation and ourselves to speak up as long as the New Moral Majority uses PC to demand silence by threat to reputation or livelihood. We must decry those who suppress us under the guise of PC. Don't allow freedom of boycott to replace freedom of speech; instead, boycott those acting to end free speech. The death of hate speech demands we use our freedom to voice hate of the speech even as we treasure others' freedom to hear it. Join me. It's time we became deplorable and proud—and, once again, free.

BIBLIOGRAPHY

(WHERE THE AUTHOR STOLE THE IDEAS WHEN HE RAN OUT OF HIS OWN)

Adams, Nick. *Retaking America: Crushing Political Correctness*. New York: Post Hill Press, 2016.

Andrews, Robert. *The Columbia Dictionary of Quotations*. New York: Columbia University Press, 1993.

Anselm of Canterbury. *Proslogion (Discourse on the Existence of God)*. 1078.

Arneson, Richard. "Egalitarianism," in *Stanford Encyclopedia of Philosophy*. Stanford CA: The Metaphysics Research Lab, Center for the Study of Language and Information, Stanford University, 2013.

Ash, Timothy Garton. *Free Speech: Ten Principles for a Connected World*. New Haven: Yale University Press, 2016.

Barnes, Jonathan, editor. *The Complete Works of Aristotle*. Princeton: Princeton University Press, 1995.

Bartlett, John. *Familiar Quotations, Fourteenth Edition*, Emily Morison Beck, Ed. Boston: Little, Brown and Company, 1968.

Blackburn, Simon. *Oxford Dictionary of Philosophy*. New York: Oxford University Press, 2008.

Bloom, Paul. *Against Empathy: The Case for Rational Compassion*. New York: HarperCollins Publishers, 2016.

Bowdler, Thomas. *The Family Shakespeare in Three Volumes: in which nothing is added to the original text; but those words and expressions are omitted which cannot with propriety be read aloud in a family. The Dramatic Works of William Shakespeare Adopted for Family Reading*. New York: Ishi Press International, 2008.

Charlton, Bruce. *Thought Prison: The Fundamental Nature of Political Correctness*. Buckingham: University of Buckingham Press, 2011.

Cook, David. *The Anatomy of Blindness*. Bloomington, Indiana: AuthorHouse, 2013.

———. *Biomythology: The Skeptic's Guide to Charles Darwin and the Science of Persuasion*. Bloomington, Indiana: AuthorHouse, 2016.

Cooper, John M., editor. *Plato Complete Works*. Indianapolis: Hackett Publishing Company, 1997.

Crane, Tim. *The Meaning of Belief: Religion from an Atheist's Point of View*. Cambridge, Massachusetts: Harvard University Press, 2017.

Cummings, E. E. *E. E. Cummings Complete Poems, 1904–1962, George Firmage, editor*. New York: Liveright Publishing Corporation, 2016.

Ereshefsky, Marc. "Species," in *Stanford Encyclopedia of Philosophy*. Stanford, CA: The Metaphysics Research Lab,

Center for the Study of Language and Information, Stanford University, 2016.

Feyerabend, Paul. *Against Method*. New York: Verso, 2010.

Fullinwider, Robert. "Affirmative Action" in *Stanford Encyclopedia of Philosophy*. Stanford CA: The Metaphysics Research Lab, Center for the Study of Language and Information, Stanford University, 2014.

Goldberg, Bernard. *Bias: A CBS Insider Exposes How the Media Distort the News*. New York: Perennial, 2003.

Grimm, Jacob and Grimm, Wilhelm. *Grimm's Complete Fairy Tales*, Translated by Margaret Hunt. New York: Barnes and Noble, 2015

Herrnstein, Richard J. and Murray, Charles. *The Bell Curve: Intelligence and Class Structure in American Life*. New York: A Free Press Paperbacks Book, 1994.

Holy Bible, Old and New Testaments in the King James Version. Nashville: Thomas Nelson, Inc., 1976.

Hughes, Geoffrey. *Political Correctness: A History of Semantics and Culture*. West Sussex: Wiley-Blackwell, 2010.

Hume, David. *A Treatise of Human Nature*. New York: Penguin Classics, 1969.

James, Michael. "Race," in *Stanford Encyclopedia of Philosophy*. Stanford, CA: The Metaphysics Research Lab, Center for the Study of Language and Information, Stanford University, 2017.

Jefferson, Thomas. *An Act for Establishing Religious Freedom*, 1786. https://www.encyclopediavirginia.org/An_Act_for_establishing_religious_Freedom_1786

Lahav, Noam. *Biogenesis: Theories of Life's Origin*. New York: Oxford University Press, 1999.

Locke, John. *Two Treatises of Government*, Edited by Peter Laslett. Cambridge: Cambridge University Press, 2016.

Machiavelli, Niccolo. *The Prince*. Hollywood, Florida: Simon & Brown, 2010.

Marx, Karl. "Introduction to a Contribution to Critique of Hegel's Philosophy of Right." *Deutsch Französishe Jahrbücher* 7 & 10 February, 1894, Paris. https://www.marxists.org/archive/marx/works/1843/critique-hpr/intro.htm

McDowell, Gary L. *Equity and the Constitution: The Supreme Court, Equitable Relief and Public Policy*. Chicago: University of Chicago Press, 1982.

Mill, John Stuart. *On Liberty*. Indianapolis: The Bobbs-Merrill Company, Inc., 1956.

Orgel, Stephen and Braunmuller, A. R., general editors. *The Complete Pelican Shakespeare*. New York: Penguin Books, 2002.

Partington, Angela. *The Oxford Dictionary of Quotations*, Revised Fourth Edition. Oxford: Oxford University Press, 1996.

Powers, Kirsten. *The Silencing: How the Left Is Killing Free Speech*. Washington, D.C.: Regnery Publishing, 2015.

Rothstein, Richard. *The Color of Law: A Forgotten History of How Our Government Segregated America*. New York: Liveright Publishing Corporation, 2017.

Rummel, R. J. *Death by Government*. New Brunswick: Transaction Publishers, 2008.

Sagan, Carl. *The Demon-Haunted World: Science as the Candle in the Dark*. New York: Ballantine Books, 1996.

Shaw, George Bernard. "Maxims for Revolutionists, 1903," in *Man and Superman: A Comedy and Philosophy*. New York: Penguin Books, 1972.

Sheed, Frank. *Theology and Sanity*. San Francisco: Ignatius Press, 1978.

Sussman, Robert Wald. *The Myth of Race: The Troubling Persistence of an Unscientific Idea*. Cambridge, Massachusetts: Harvard University Press, 2014.

Swift, Jonathan. *A Modest Proposal and Other Prose*. New York: Barnes and Noble, 2004.

Twain, Mark. *Adventure of Huckleberry Finn (Tom Sawyer's Comrade)*. New York: Charles L. Webster and Company, 1885.

Twain, Mark. *Mark Twain Quotations,* Barbara Schmidt, editor. www.twainquotes.com

Twain, Mark and Gribben, Alan. *Adventure of Huckleberry Finn, NewSouth Edition*. Montgomery, Alabama: NewSouth Books, 2011.

Washington, Booker T. *Up From Slavery: An Autobiography*. New York: Doubleday, Page, & Co., 1907.

————. *My Larger Education: Being Chapters from My Experience*. Garden City, New York: Doubleday, Page and Company, 1911.

Washington, Harriett A. *Medical Apartheid: The Dark History of Medical Experimentation on Black American from Colonial Times to the Present*. New York: Harlem Books, 2006.

Whitman, Walt. *Leaves of Grass*. New York: The Modern Library, 1993.

Wills, Gary. "Lincoln's Black History." *The New York Review of Books*: 56(10). June 11, 2009.

Wilson, A. N. *Hitler*. New York: Basic Books, 2012.

Wittgenstein, Ludwig. *Philosophical Investigations*. West Sussex: Wiley-Blackwell, 2009.

Yale Law School. *The Avalon Project: Documents in Law, History, and Diplomacy*. New Haven, CT: Lillian Goldman Law Library, 2008.

ACKNOWLEDGMENTS

Just in case anyone reads this far, before we go, some acknowledgments are out of order. (I should have put them at the beginning of the book so readers would have known from the get-go who to blame for these mean-spirited pages.)

Thanks to all conservative intellectuals for enjoying this book: both of you.

To Dr. Robert Sanet, for sending me all these darn Occupy Democrats posts on Facebook, infuriating me until I ran out of room and had to respond with a book. Dr. Sanet is greatly admired by his peers, including me, and has more friends in our profession than anyone I know. Still, no one is perfect, and befriending me (and inspiring this book) will remain one of Dr. Sanet's greatest blunders. Sorry, Bob.

To Dr. Dominick Maino, for reviewing as much of my book as he could stomach. Overall, he felt the book would have been better if I had written it in English and he deleted most of my ideas. Still Dr. Maino admitted the book made him think—while he was asleep. ("Gave me nightmares," as he put it.) Thank you, Dom.

To Sandra Kay Koch, for reading the manuscript and convincing me how brilliant I am. (Sandra Kay works for me, of course. I would have fired her for saying anything less.)

To Cheryl Molin, for editing the book. Never has an editor done more with less. Still, because I had the final say in everything, readers can hardly blame Cheryl for my errors. I'll blame her, but readers can't.

And most of all, for my beautiful wife, who was temporarily widowed as I wrestled to reconcile the manuscript with human decency—and failed.

CONTACTING THE AUTHOR

Please address all love letters, hate mail, comments, and critiques to David Cook at drcook2020@gmail.com. Explosive devices—send those to Madonna. Her quoted politically correct dreams for the White House do not reflect the author's opinion any more than do the words of this book.

ENDNOTES

PREFACE

1. Note well: The "values" of the politically correct just got voted in for "the people of the United States."

2. Oct. 6, 2017 letter to Hon. Donald J. Trump, President; Hon. Mitch McConell, Majority Leader; Hon. Paul Ryan, Speaker. In Art Moore, "War on Free-Speech: Conservatives Warn Trump of Hate Measure: 'Open-Ended' Mandate by Congress 'Invites Abuses of Power by State.'" 10/7/17. http://www.wnd.com/author/amoore-com/?archive=true.

INTRODUCTION

1. Robert Andrews, *The Columbia Dictionary of Quotations* (New York: Columbia University Press, 1993), 710.

CHAPTER 1

1. Niccolo Machiavelli, *The Prince* (Hollywood, Florida: Simon & Brown, 2010), 66.

2. According to 1860 census data, only 384,884 out of 31,443,321 Americans, or less than 2 percent, were "slave holders." Since then, tens of millions of immigrants, with no participation in slavery, have arrived. Few alive in America today had ancestors who were slave holders. Numbers, of course, lie; statistics sell politics, not truth. What percentage of Americans tacitly supported slavery by their votes or by drinking rum or wearing cotton underwear just as

today we support laws allowing the import of clothing produced for slave wages in third-world countries? Nothing has changed. Instead of looking in the mirror, we continue to blame our failures on our ancestors or rivals.

3.   To take this remark out of the realm of prose and place it in the realm of perception, search "Selective attention test—YouTube." http:/www.youtube.com/watch?v=vJG698U2Mvo.

4.   I'm not claiming that homosexuality is somehow more perverse than fornication, evil thoughts, slander, foolishness or abortion, but I remain unconvinced that moral truth is best defined by grassroots politics or the temporal groupthink of Supreme Court justices.

5.   In the *Phaedrus*, Plato's favorite protagonist Socrates coined "carve nature at the joints" to describe "kinds" that are really to be found in nature. A *dog* is a "kind." It has real, natural boundaries that discourage it from kissing cats or asses. *Gold* is a "kind." It has real, natural boundaries. It is not lead or hogwash. Political and emotional terms are not *kinds* with exact boundaries, but they allow us to imagine we are communicating with one another. Where does socialism end and communism begin? Where does production end and poverty begin? What exactly divides *dyslexia* from *poopy reading*? The experts, not nature, do the voting. In these essays, I will argue that terms like *racism* and *xenophobia* are more like *poopy reading* than *gold*. Concocted from groupthink, such political terms carve our emotions; they do not "carve nature at the joints."

6.   In the words of writer James Baldwin, "*Whoever debases others is debasing himself.* That is not a mystical statement but a most realistic one, which is proved by the eyes of any Alabama sheriff—and I would not like to see Negroes ever arrive at so wretched a condition [Baldwin's italics]." Quoted in Timothy Garton Ash, *Free Speech: Ten Principles for a Connected World* (New Haven: Yale University Press, 2016), 89.

7. George Bernard Shaw, "Maxims for Revolutionists, 1903," in *Man and Superman: A Comedy and Philosophy* (New York: Penguin Books, 1972), 251.

8. In Lincoln's words, "Certainly the negro is not our equal in color—perhaps not in many respects; still, in the right to put into his mouth the bread that his own hands have earned, he is the equal of every other man, white or black." Lincoln was a coon-joke-telling bigot, who objected to slavery because it unfairly lowered the wages of competing whites. See Gary Wills, "Lincoln's Black History." *The New York Review of Books*: 56(10). June, 11, 2009.

CHAPTER 2

1. Both optometrists and ophthalmologists are licensed to examine eyes, but optometrists, like dentists, belong to a profession independent from, and not directly controlled by, organized medicine.

2. Sorry folks. Other than in footnote 1, I will not refer to the supremacists by name. You do not see Coca Cola wasting their advertising budget increasing Pepsi's name recognition with a "Pepsi Ain't It" slogan. Only journalistic morons would take every opportunity to turn the name of their competitor into a household word.

3. When Your Child Struggles: The Myths of 20/20 Vision: What Every Parent Needs to Know (Atlanta: Invision Press, 1992). I am careful not to autograph the copies, lest their value drop on eBay.

4. "Raindrops Keep Falling on My Head." Hal David wrote the words; Burt Bacharach, music. The philosophy could be countered with, "Get an umbrella." Political correctness is indeed an *umbrella* term used to justify the need to censor political rivals.

5. Morons at Oxford. Some are agitating for gender-neutral pronouns such as "ze" instead of "he" or "she" so as not to cue transgender

students into intuiting they might be different. Changing the language of Charles Dickens and Emily Dickinson to assuage less than 2 percent of the population makes about as much sense as dumbing down Shakespeare until he can be grasped by those with IQs of 70. Equality demands it. A couple standard deviations from the mean are a couple standard deviations. If the deviants are on Einstein's end of the bell curve, they'll be smart enough not to require the accommodation. If they share the end of the curve with the less fortunate, that may be a different matter.

6. You needn't be politically correct here; supply your own.

7. Washingtonpost.com/news/volokh-conspiracy/wp/2017/01/21/ no-madonnas-i-have-thought-an-awful-lot-about-blowing-up-the-white-house-isnt-a-threat-of-violence//utm_term=.aedd257b60ba

CHAPTER 3

1. Ed Crews, "Rattle-Skull, Stonewall, Bogus, Blackstrap, Bombo, Mimbo, Whistle Belly, Syllabub, Sling, Toddy, and Flip: Drinking in Colonial America," History.org/foundation/journal/holiday07/drink.cfm

2. John Stuart Mill, *On Liberty* (Indianapolis: The Bobbs-Merrill Company, Inc., 1956), 39.

3. Yes, it was 1968, and the parents would most likely have referred to themselves as "blacks." Jesse Jackson didn't popularize "African American," placing descent before nation, for another twenty years, although according to the Oxy Morons, *African American* entered the language as early as 1782: "That the ruler of the universe may crown with success the cause of freedom, and speedily relieve your bleeding country, is the hearty wish of an African American."

4. Racist.

5. Niccolo Machiavelli, *The Prince* (Hollywood, Florida: Simon & Brown, 2010), 66.

6. Doris Lessing, *Sunday Times: Books,* London 10 May 1992 in Robert Andrews, *The Columbia Dictionary of Quotations* (New York: Columbia University Press 1993), 702.

7. Geoffrey Hughes, *Political Correctness: A History of Semantics and Culture* (West Sussex: Wiley-Blackwell, 2010), 16.

8. What is communism? In Chapter 2 of the *Communist Manifesto* (1848) Karl Marx and Friedrich Engels wrote, "The theory of the communists may be summed up in a single sentence: Abolition of private property." More specifically—abolition of someone else's private property. It's fine to abolish the authorship of a business or factory but not the authorship of a book. The *Communist Manifesto,* for instance, is not attributed to "The People."

9. Doris Lessing in (Hughes 2010), p. 13.

10. The "veto" idea I stole, like many others, from Timothy Garton Ashe's remarkably balanced and well-written book *Free Speech: Ten Principles for a Connected World* (New Haven: Yale University Press, 2017). It's true that Ashe is an Oxy Moron, which I suppose reduces me to an Atlanta idiot—were I trying to be consistent. Which I'm not.

CHAPTER 4

1. Friedrich Nietzsche, *Beyond Good and Evil*, Aphorism 146. Free eBooks At Planet eBook.com, 91. Planetebook.com/ebooks/Beyond-Good-and-Evil.pdf.

2. Jonathan Leader Maynard, Susan Benesch (2016) "Dangerous Speech and Dangerous Ideology: An Integrated Model for Monitoring and Prevention," *Genocide Studies and Prevention: An*

International Journal: Vol. 9: Iss. 3: 70–95. DOI: http://dx.doi. org/10.5038/1911-9933.9.3.1317

3. All parenthetical additions in this paragraph are my own.

4. When a bigoted idiot murders a liberal protestor, the press cries, "Ban Bigotry!" When a liberal idiot attempts to murder a conservative congressman, does the press cry, "Ban Liberalism"? Perhaps we should condemn the violent idiots rather than use them as excuses to ban freedom of speech? Perhaps we should forbid illegal actions, not unpopular ideologies? Perhaps, not. We'll consider such questions in subsequent chapters.

5. Timothy Garton Ash, *Free Speech: Ten Principles for a Connected World* (New Haven: Yale University Press, 2016), 150.

6. R. J. Rummel, *Death by Government* (New Brunswick: Transaction Publishers, 2008).

7. A. N. Wilson, *Hitler* (New York: Basic Books, 2012), 187.

CHAPTER 5

1. Paul Feyerabend, *Against Method* (New York: Verso, 2010), 7.

2. Using U.S. Center for Disease Control and Prevention data, there have been at least forty-three million abortions performed since 1973, the year of the *Roe v. Wade* Supreme Court decision. See www.christianliferesponse.com.

3. In Mark 7:21–22, Jesus describes some evil things that come from within and defile the man. These include, among others, evil thoughts, adulteries, fornications, murders, lasciviousness (lust), blasphemy (slander), and even foolishness. Jesus makes no attempt to separate the bad no-no's from the less bad no-no's. We all sin. My goal in this essay is not to distinguish homosexuals as being

better sinners than the rest of us; I am doubtful, however, that grass-root politics or political action committees or groupthink—or laws themselves—have any power to redefine sin. I would argue that Christians—even the foolish ones like myself who sometimes think bad thoughts—have no moral obligation to reclassify homosexuality or fornication as worthy of parades.

4. Kirsten Powers, *The Silencing: How the Left Is Killing Free Speech* (Washington, D.C.: Regnery Publishing, 2015), 49–51.

5. Chapter 1, definitions 1 *and* 2.

6. As long as we are not blind to the color of the past.

CHAPTER 6

1. As Carl Sagan described witch hunts in *The Demon-Haunted World: Science as a Candle in the Dark* (New York: Ballantine Books, 1996), 119: "Little attention is given to the possibility that accusations might be made for impious purposes—jealousy, say, or revenge, or the greed of the inquisitors who routinely confiscated for their own private benefit the property of the accused."

2. https://www.celebritynetworth.com/richest-celebrities/actor/bill-cosby-net-worth

3. http://www.eightcitiesmap.com/transcript_bc.htm

4. http://www.washingtontimes.com/news/2004/sep/9/20040909-121926-4474r/

5. Alan Brownfield, Ibid.

6. Booker T. Washington, *My Larger Education: Being Chapters from My Experience* (Garden City, New York: Doubleday, Page and Company, 1911), 118.

7. Brian Logan, "It Took a Comedian to Call Bill Cosby to Account," https://www.theguardian.com/stage/2014/nov/26/Hannibal-buress-bill-cosby-comedy-taboo

CHAPTER 7

1. To lie under oath or defraud others would obviously not be justified under the heading of "free speech," but there also comes a point when debaters and consumers have to beware. (Where exactly that point is we'll leave open to debate, should the politically correct allow the debate.) To force businesses to waste billions of dollars on printing warnings to protect those who somehow avoided institutionalization but never figured out that coffee is hot (and pass on the printing costs and legal fees to consumers) is folly trying to extinguish folly. As a fool, I'm always happy to have the company, of course, but playing the fool does not require imagining vast armies of those more foolish than I am. I'll save that for the elite.

2. O. J. may have gotten away with murder in this world, but let's hope we don't all get what we deserve in the next, that Jesus's opinion of our salvation lives up to our own exaggerated expectations. That the family of the characters in O. J.'s book got the literary proceeds should please anyone judging a man who has spent his life trying to go to jail. We can only pray that O. J. will see the light, and the angels will rejoice. We can only pray that the adulterous characters in O. J.'s book also saw the light. Imagine the irony of O. J. having a happier eternity than his alleged victims, not to mention equally sinful fools such as me.

3. Joy Peskin, "Drawing the Line," *Publisher's Weekly*, February 6, 2016, p. 72.

4. Capitalism, not sodomy or fornication, being politically incorrect.

5. Boycott actually IS a form of freedom of speech, and I will whole-heartedly recommend boycott by the end of this chapter. Using boycott to encourage freedom of speech, however, is different than using boycott to prevent others from being heard, which is more like shouting down a speaker from the back of an auditorium—also an example of "free speech." Using freedom of speech to refute an argument is different than using freedom of speech to avoid having to refute an argument.

6. Caroline Mala Corbin, "The First Amendment Right Against Compelled Listening," *Boston University Law Review,* 2009: vol. 89, 939–1016.

7. We can't be sure the sheep would agree, but sheep haven't organized politically to carve out pastoral turf.

8. Sexual longing for mid to late adolescents. Since adolescence ends when we become self-supporting, this philia takes in quite an age range, for it includes the victims of social welfare projects that allowed the victims never to grow up.

9. πϱόβατο or *próvato* is Greek for "sheep," Greek being preferred by the NMM when coining politically incorrect transgressions.

10. David Hume, *A Treatise of Human Nature* (New York: Penguin Classics, 1969), Volume II, Book II, Section III.

11. Booker T. Washington, *Up From Slavery: An Autobiography* (New York: Doubleday, Page, & Co., 1907), 165.

12. Timothy Garton Ash, *Free Speech: Ten Principles for a Connected World* (New Haven: Yale University Press, 2016), Part II, Chapter 2.

13. See "In U.S., More Adults Identifying as LGBT." Gallup (report) January 11, 2017 and https://www.cnbc.com/.../a-record-number-of-americans-are-now-millionaires-new-study-shows.html

14. Excusing our own responsibility by blaming our parents and environments, nature and nurture.

15. The analogy is obviously false; those who continue to repeat the "right" homicides are not "serial killers," at least not as the term is used today. Not since shortly after Eden's doors closed has a state existed without the threat of, need for, or fallout from, war. But the pain of those losing loved ones to homicide persists. It is generally wise, I imagine, to reexamine our interpretations of words before killing others' loved ones in the name of Jesus. Romans 13:1 has, for instance, been used to justify living by rulers' swords despite any cautions Jesus gave about living by our own swords: "Let every soul be subject unto the higher powers. For there is no power but of God: the powers that be are ordained of God." Hitler's army probably loved the passage. I'll let the theologians work out the connection between "higher powers" and Roe v. Wade.

16. This, of course, is tongue in cheek. People don't "decide" to stand in their seats for a better view rather than to trample others. Trampling is done, not by one person making a decision, but a mob panicking. Free will is always trampled by groupthink. So, what's new?

17. *Areopagitica*, 1644.

18. John Stuart Mill, *On Liberty* (Indianapolis: The Bobbs-Merrill Company, Inc., 1956), 21.

19. This quote and the rest of the James Madison quotes come from "The Same Subject Continued: The Union as a Safeguard Against Domestic Faction and Insurrection. From the New York Packet." Friday, November 23, 1787. The Federalist Papers: No. 10. Avalon. law.yale.edu.

20. For the philosopher John Locke, who heavily influenced our Founding Fathers, our most basic rights were "life, liberty, and the pursuit of property."

21. In a "true democracy" the citizens all get together to personally vote on each issue.

22. "Curt Schilling, ESPN Analyst, Is Fired Over Offensive Social Media Post," *New York Times,* April 20, 2016. https://nyti.ms/20YQ9bO

23. Ibid.

24. David Cole, "Why We Must Still Defend Free Speech," *The New York Review of Books,* Sept. 28, 2017, pp. 61–62.

CHAPTER 8

1. One of those limitations to freedom of speech, as we noted in the previous chapter.

2. Anselm of Canterbury, *Proslogion (Discourse on the Existence of God),* 1078.

3. Throughout this polemic, I subscribe to absolute truth when speaking of God. When speaking of PC, I fallaciously subscribe to sophistry, for in PC two wrongs always make a right—the wrongs of the past justify the wrongs of the present. As a good sophist, my only job is to make the sale. Readers who trust in God should (and will) discount anything I write that diverges in any manner from their understanding of biblical teaching. Readers who trust in secularism may accept or reject my sophistry, using the same relative standards they use to justify or condemn everything else, replacing a personal God with a personal truth.

CHAPTER 9

1. For a balanced treatment of egalitarianism see Richard Arneson, "Egalitarianism," in *Stanford Encyclopedia of Philosophy* (Stanford, CA: The Metaphysics Research Lab, Center for the Study of Language and Information, Stanford University, 2013).. Philosophers, like

clowns on unicycles, must appear to be balanced. Polemicists, present company included, need not.

2. Karl Marx, "Introduction to a Contribution to Critique of Hegel's Philosophy of Right," *Deutsch Französishe Jahrbücher* February7 & 10, 1894, Paris. https://www.marxists.org/archive/marx/works/1843/critique-hpr/intro.htm

3. Filicide is the killing of children by their parents.

4. This, of course, is not always the case. Some families are run according to the wisdom of three-year-olds. Or the children receive intensive sales and rape training, learning that "no," with enough persistence, screaming, and threats can always be turned into "yes."

5. It's certainly my favorite rhetorical tool. See David Cook, *Biomythology: The Skeptic's Guide to Charles Darwin and the Science of Persuasion* (Bloomington, Indiana: AuthorHouse), 2016, for a complete treatment of how to use science for the purpose of sales to naïve philosophers or the lay public.

6. *Proper Studies*, "The Idea of Equality," in Robert Andrews, *The Columbia Dictionary of Quotations* (New York: Columbia University Press, 1993), 285.

7. And providentially, the right to vengeance requires playing with a full deck.

8. John Bartlett, *Familiar Quotations, Fourteenth Edition,* Emily Morison Beck, Ed. (Boston: Little, Brown and Company, 1968), 125.

9. LXXX Sermons (1640) 8 March1621/2 in Angela Partington, *The Oxford Dictionary of Quotations*, Revised Fourth Edition (Oxford: Oxford University Press, 1996), 253.

10. Robert Andrews, *The Columbia Dictionary of Quotations* (New York: Columbia University Press, 1993), 284.

11. If you are a liberal, the genius/idiot example may seem deplorable. Another way to put this is that since Democrats are wise and Republicans are stupid, and it is easier to make a wise person stupid than a stupid person wise, equality demands we all become Republicans. Or not?

12. Not that Jefferson was delusional enough to imagine that all were equal on his property.

CHAPTER 10

1. "And the Lord God said, It is not good that the man should be alone." (Genesis 2:18)

2. John Locke, *Two Treatises of Government*, Edited by Peter Laslett (Cambridge: Cambridge University Press, 2016), 297–88

3. Deplorables have been viewed as a variety of nut. Still, they are never property. They have property rights of their own, despite the teachings of those who dehumanize us.

4. Well actually Locke isn't referring to anything. He is now equal with all the other dead men. And the universal solvent of rhetorical reason can be used to stretch Locke's perception of property to reach even our passion for the theme of relationship in this essay.

5. Richard Rothstein, *The Color of Law: A Forgotten History of How Our Government Segregated America* (New York: Liveright Publishing Corporation, 2017),vii-viii.

CHAPTER 11

1. Whether this is a mixed metaphor or juxtaposed scientific viewpoints, I will leave for you to decide.

2. I'm not about to commit blasphemy and join Salman Rushdie on the hitlist of those voted least likely to succeed. I'm probably already in enough trouble with the New Moral Majority to risk the ire of another group of religious zealots.

3. http://www.statisticbrain.com/prostitution-statistics/ downloaded 4/9/2017.

4. http://www.statisticbrain.com/legal-occupation-salary-statistics downloaded 10/27/17.

CHAPTER 12

1. This essay says next to nothing about quotas. I am mimicking Internet headlines that often say nothing about their articles. The typical headline reads, "Trump Commits Atrocity Against Humanity." The article itself mentions no actual atrocity and turns out to be about liberals, not humanity.

2. David Cook, *Biomythology: The Skeptic's Guide to Charles Darwin and the Science of Persuasion* (Bloomington, Indiana: AuthorHouse, 2016). 10.

3. Thomas Henry Huxley, "Mr. Darwin's Critics" 1871 in *Collected Essays, Volume II, Darwiniana* (London: Macmillan and Company, 1893), 165.

4. See Noam Lahav, *Biogenesis: Theories of Life's Origin* (New York: Oxford University Press, 1999) for the disagreements on the definition of "life" (James 2017), for disagreements on the definition of "race," and (Ereshefsky 2016) for disagreements on the definition of "species." Indeed, Jody Hey in ("The mind species problem," Trends in Ecology and Evolution, July 2001) lists two dozen definitions of "species."

5. Daniel J. Fairbanks, *Everyone Is African: How Science Explodes the Myth of Race* (Amherst, N.Y.: Prometheus, 2015), . 11.

6. The statements qualify as expert opinion but only if we imagine Fairbanks majored in genetics and minored in white supremacy. His pronouncements are about as dependable as those of an optometrist writing on PC—although PC is largely about the perversion of language, and the optometrist majored in English at UCLA.

7. Booker T. Washington, *My Larger Education: Being Chapters from My Experience* (Garden City, New York: Doubleday, Page and Company, 1911), 118.

8. Booker T. *Up From Slavery: An Autobiography* (New York: Doubleday, Page, & Co., 1907), 165.

9. Ibid.

10. *Shorter Oxford English Dictionary* (Oxford: Oxford University Press, 2007).

11. http://www.independent.co.uk/news/science/fury-at-dna-pioneers-theory-africans-are-less-intelligent-than-westerner-394898.html.

12. https://www.nytimes.com/2016/08/21/magazine/the-easiest-way-to-get-rid-of-racism-just-redefine-it.html

13. Saldana lights up the screen whatever role she plays. She'd be one of my favorite actresses whether she were purple, white, or gold. Her talent transcends color to make her irresistible whatever race or species she plays. Her biography describes her as an American, no modifier required.

14. To listen to the recording of the conversation, visit www.youtube.com and search for "Clippers Owner Donald Sterling to Girlfriend: Don't Bring Black People to My Games."

15. I intend to use the same press agent to illustrate my relationship to this book. As earlier stated, it does not reflect my views, and certainly not my actions.

16. Simon Blackburn, *Oxford Dictionary of Philosophy* (New York: Oxford University Press, 2008), 196.

17. Slavery need not be justified by skin-think. In the ancient world, slavery was justified as part of the spoils of war. Losers were enslaved—indeed, Africans used this "spoils" justification, not skin-think, to justify enslaving and selling their fellow Africans. These victors were traders, not racists—by our definition.

18. Harriett A. Washington, *Medical Apartheid: The Dark History of Medical Experimentation on Black American from Colonial Times to the Present* (New York: Harlem Books, 2006.)

19. Actually, white supremacists, according to the politically correct, are all terrorists. Only terror, not illusions of grandeur, qualifies one as a white supremacist. General Washington was certainly guilty of both terror and violence, but only against the British. He was not a supremacist; he was quite simply a racist, using skin-think to justify the status quo of his day.

20. When it comes to terror, fear of loss of life certainly trumps fear of loss of livelihood, but without including the breaking of laws against violence and homicide, the Facebook page example could be more devastating. The r-word can destroy a life without the need to break any law.

21. *Oxford English Dictionary*, on line, viewed 10/19/17.

22. Matthew 13:13.

CHAPTER 13

1. David Cook, *Biomythology: The Skeptic's Guide to Charles Darwin and the Science of Persuasion* (Bloomington, Indiana: AuthorHouse, 2016), 12.

2. Thomas Bowdler, *The Family Shakespeare in Three Volumes: in which nothing is added to the original text; but those words and expressions*

are omitted which cannot with propriety be read aloud in a family. The Dramatic Works of William Shakespeare Adopted for Family Reading. New York: Ishi Press International, 2008.

3. Although children may guide us to enter the Kingdom of Heaven, they are no certain guides to logic or the kingdom of Caesar. Indeed, their minds are not developed to think logically until they are nearly in their teens. Then puberty strikes and they are overwhelmed by hormones for another forty years. Still, I would not suggest that parents be raised by their children—even if political correctness is eager to manufacture "childhood rights" to move us in that direction.

4. Robert Hughes, *Culture of Complaint* (New York: Warner Books, 1993), 18-19.

5. David Cook, *Biomythology: The Skeptic's Guide to Charles Darwin and the Science of Persuasion* (Bloomington, Indiana: AuthorHouse, 2016), xii.)

6. To "expurgate" is to censure or remove the naughty parts, the only reasons you are reading the text in the first place.

7. Mark Twain and Alan Gribben, *Adventure of Huckleberry Finn, NewSouth Edition.* (Montgomery, AL: NewSouth Books, 2011), p. xxiv.

8. Ibid., 31.

CHAPTER 14

1. In 1910, the term *moron*, itself, was coined to turn stupidity into a science by prominent psychologist and eugenicist H. H. Goddard: "The other (suggestion) is to call them [feeble-minded children] by the Greek word 'moron'. It is defined as one who is lacking in intelligence, one who is deficient in judgement or sense." OED. I use the Greek term *moron* to appear both "scientific" and offensive.

2. The name rhymes with "hot," not "dough"although we can hope, after her recent spectacular success, she will soon be rolling in it.

CHAPTER 15

1. Whatever exactly these terms may mean. To call someone a murderer or an adulterer may or may not be a slur. If, however, we include anyone who has ever had an unkind thought toward a member of another race or sex, then racist, sexist may mean nothing more than being human, a thing-hater in a world in which everyone hates something.

2. Do as I say, not as I do.

CHAPTER 16

1. To "emerge from" is to be greater than the sum of the parts. The mind emerges from the brain just as Niagara Falls emerges from hydrogen and oxygen. We cannot find the mind counting nerve cells; we cannot find Niagara Falls counting water molecules; nor can we find Truth counting viewpoints. Pluralism rests on the sum of its equal parts. Emergence imagines no such equality of parts, just that even the false parts bring the truth into greater relief, greater perspective—as Mill argued in our "Freedom of Silence" chapter.

2. John Stuart Mill, *On Liberty* (Indianapolis: The Bobbs-Merrill Company, Inc., 1956), 25.

3. Walt Whitman, *Leaves of Grass* (New York: The Modern Library, 1993), 35.

4. Paul Feyerabend, *Against Method* (New York: Verso, 2010), 14.

5. Jonathan Swift, *A Modest Proposal and Other Prose* (New York: Barnes and Noble, 2004).

 WORLD AHEAD *press*

Authors welcome! Publishing your book with us means that you have the freedom to blaze your own trail. But that doesn't mean you should go it alone. By choosing to publish with WORLD AHEAD PRESS, you partner with WND—one of the most powerful and influential brands on the Internet.

If you liked this book and want to publish your own, WORLD AHEAD PRESS, co-publishing division of WND Books, is right for you. WORLD AHEAD PRESS will turn your manuscript into a high-quality book and then promote it through its broad reach into conservative and Christian markets worldwide.

IMAGINE YOUR BOOK ALONGSIDE THESE AUTHORS!

We transform your manuscript into a marketable book. Here's what you get:

BEAUTIFUL CUSTOM BOOK COVER
PROFESSIONAL COPYEDIT
INTERIOR FORMATTING
EBOOK CONVERSION
KINDLE EBOOK EDITION
WORLDWIDE BOOKSTORE DISTRIBUTION
MARKETING ON AMAZON.COM

It's time to publish your book with WORLD AHEAD PRESS.

Go to www.worldaheadpress.com for a Free Consultation

CPSIA information can be obtained
at www.ICGtesting.com
Printed in the USA
BVOW08s2223190318
511022BV00001B/72/P